FIND
YOUR
GODDESS

FIND
YOUR
GODDESS

How to Manifest the Power and Wisdom of the Ancient Goddesses in Your Everyday Life

SKYE
ALEXANDER

ADAMS MEDIA

NEW YORK LONDON TORONTO SYDNEY NEW DELHI

Adams Media
An Imprint of Simon & Schuster, LLC
100 Technology Center Drive
Stoughton, Massachusetts 02072

First Adams Media trade paperback edition JANUARY 2018

ADAMS MEDIA and colophon are trademarks of Simon and Schuster.

For information about special discounts for bulk purchases, please contact Simon & Schuster Special Sales at 1-866-506-1949 or business@simonandschuster.com.

The Simon & Schuster Speakers Bureau can bring authors to your live event. For more information or to book an event contact the Simon & Schuster Speakers Bureau at 1-866-248-3049 or visit our website at www.simonspeakers.com.

Interior design by Katrina Machado
Image credits listed at the end of this book, except interior images on openers © iStockphoto.com/-1001-; Shutterstock/vextor studio

Manufactured in China

10 9 8 7 6 5

Library of Congress Cataloging-in-Publication Data
Alexander, Skye, author.
Find your goddess / Skye Alexander.
Avon, Massachusetts: Adams Media, 2018.
LCCN 2017037303 (print) | LCCN 2017045315 (ebook) | ISBN 9781507205297 (pb) | ISBN 9781507205303 (ebook)
LCSH: Goddess religion. | Goddesses.
LCC BL473.5 (ebook) | LCC BL473.5 .A46 2018 (print) | DDC 202/.114--dc23
LC record available at https://lccn.loc.gov/2017037303

ISBN 978-1-5072-0529-7
ISBN 978-1-5072-0530-3 (ebook)

DEDICATION

To all the goddesses in my life: my many
women friends, my sisters Myke
and Laurie, my nieces Morgan and Ryan,
and my Bast-in-residence Zoe.

ACKNOWLEDGMENTS

It takes a village to make a book, and in this case that means the amazingly talented and enterprising staff at Adams Media. I especially want to thank my editor Eileen Mullan for her inspired vision and ongoing support, Frank Rivera, Katrina Machado, and Michelle Kelly for their gorgeous design, and everyone else who contributed to this book's success. You're the best!

CONTENTS

➤ • ◄

INTRODUCTION

"The Goddess is now returning. Denied and suppressed for thousands of years of masculine domination, she comes at a time of dire need....Here mythology unexpectedly comes to our aid."
—Edward C. Whitmont, *Return of the Goddess*

Long before written texts and the ascent of the organized religions we know today, the Goddess reigned over all life on earth. She provided her people with food and other necessities; she protected them during birth and death; she guided them in love and war; she taught them art, music, and law. Mythology tells us that the Goddess also formed heaven and earth. In short, the Goddess governed every facet of human existence.

One of the oldest artifacts shaped by human hands is the Venus of Willendorf, a 25,000-year-old figurine of a female that anthropologists suggest may represent a mother/fertility goddess. Archaeologists have also unearthed other goddess artwork from ancient Egypt, Greece, China, and elsewhere. These, along with millennias-old literary works such as the Vedas and the *Epic of Gilgamesh*, provide information about widespread goddess worship through the ages.

REDISCOVERING HERSTORY

In modern times, we're rediscovering "herstory"—or history viewed from the female perspective. Through this lens we understand the past in a new way and, more specifically, how that past is relevant to our present.

Early cultures were polytheistic, and their legends describe thousands of goddesses, some benevolent and nurturing, others frightening and cruel. It's safe to say there was a deity associated with each and every thing in the known universe. Goddess myths reveal our ancestors' concepts of the cosmos; their desires, fears, and values; and the ongoing drama of life on earth. In this book you'll meet some of these goddesses and discover their stories. You'll also learn ways to petition the goddesses for assistance and honor them in your everyday life, for they are every bit as real today as they were millennia ago.

As you read the myths recounted in this book, you'll see goddesses dealing with the same concerns, challenges, and conundrums that still face us today. You'll witness Hera's jealousy, Sedna's betrayal, Demeter's grief, Rhiannon's unfair punishment. And you'll marvel at their bravery, wisdom, and compassion.

As you reconnect with the goddesses, you'll learn ways to draw upon their powers to cope with your dysfunctional family, the demands of your job, your unsatisfying love life, and the other ups and downs you're experiencing. Whatever your need or purpose, you'll find a goddess who can lend a hand.

The Goddess never left us and she never will. She's still guiding, protecting, and inspiring you, healing your wounds and spurring your courage. She's here right beside you, inside you, at this very moment. All you have to do is call her name and she'll answer.

GODDESS IN MYTH AND LEGEND

"I have called on the Goddess and found her within myself."
—Marion Zimmer Bradley, *The Mists of Avalon*

Throughout history, virtually every culture has entertained visions of a heavenly realm populated by beings with supernatural powers. These divine beings were said to watch over the earth and guide human destiny. They also explained natural forces, such as floods and volcanoes, that the ancients couldn't comprehend otherwise.

As our ancestors grappled with the mysteries of existence, they invented myths about the deities who governed everything on earth and in the heavens. The earliest myths described great goddesses who brought the world into being and fertility goddesses who made the crops grow, as well as goddesses who ruled the wind, rain, rivers, and mountains. Over time, the deities' roles and characteristics evolved just as human beings evolved. Goddesses guided hunters, warriors, and seafarers; they offered marital advice and delivered babies; they inspired artists, musicians, and poets; they shepherded the dead into the afterlife.

THE GODDESS PERSONIFIED

Since ancient times, people have ascribed to goddesses the characteristics they connected with women. Not surprisingly, myths talk about goddesses of love, beauty, creativity, motherhood, fertility, healing, compassion, protection, and wisdom. However, legends also tell of fierce warrior deities, such as Egypt's Sekhmet and the Celts' Badb, and terrifying rulers of the underworld, such as the Sumerians' Ereshkigal and the Norse Hel. In her book *Goddesses in Everywoman*, Jean Shinoda Bolen, MD, explains, "Myths and fairytales are expressions of archetypes....The presence of common archetypal patterns accounts for the similarities in the mythologies of many cultures."

Perhaps the most profound and omnipresent symbol of the divine feminine is Mother Earth herself. We see the earth personified as a goddess in all cultures—the Greeks knew her as Gaia, the Inca as Pachamama. Moon goddesses abound in mythology too, for the moon has long been associated with women's reproductive cycles and considered the sun's feminine counterpart.

Frequently a goddess plays more than one role. For example, some blend love and fertility whereas others are both protectors and mothers. We even find goddesses whose natures and responsibilities seem contradictory, such as the creator-destroyer deities Pele, Kali, Anuket, and Tiamat, whose dual nature represents the ongoing cycle of birth, death, and rebirth. Hindu mythology considers all goddesses to be aspects of Devi, the feminine force of the universe.

Whatever she's called, however her story is told, the Divine Feminine abides everywhere and in all of us, men as well as women.

DIVINE GODDESS COMBINATIONS

Goddesses often symbolize the three stages of a woman's life: maiden, mother, and elder. In mythology we see what's known as the Triple Goddess, a trio of deities who depict these stages. In Greek myths, we have Persephone, Demeter, and Hecate; Branwen, Cerridwen, and the Cailleach in Celtic legends; and Yemaya, Oshun, and Oya in Yoruban folklore. Myths also link the goddess trinity with the waxing, full, and waning phases of the moon.

It is common to see moon goddesses and sun gods paired in some way—the Greeks' Selene and Helios, for example—for the two heavenly bodies symbolize the feminine and masculine forces in the cosmos. Mythological marriages often pair an earth goddess with a sky god, as is the case of the Greeks' Gaia (earth) and Ouranos (sky) and of the Yoruban's Odudua (earth) and Olorun (sky). In the Egyptian pantheon, however, the goddess Nut rules the sky and her husband Geb governs the earth. Over time, stories of these divine unions have gotten muddied. According to various accounts, a goddess's consort may also be her brother, father, or son.

Sometimes goddesses are paired in myths to represent two sides of the psyche—the outer, conscious side and the darker, hidden side. The Sumerian story of Inanna and her sister Ereshkigal is one such depiction, as is Egypt's myth of Isis and Nephthys. In some legends, one goddess symbolizes life and the other death.

HOW DO GODDESSES REVEAL THEMSELVES?

How can you meet a goddess? Myths and legends from many cultures tell tales of these feminine deities interacting with humans. Such appearances aren't just a thing of the past or the province of mystics—they can happen to anyone, anytime.

Frequently, deities communicate with us through dreams. While sleeping, you're more receptive than you are in your ordinary waking state, which allows goddesses to slip you messages. Try keeping a dream journal to record any lingering thoughts you have when you wake. You may also meet a goddess during meditation. Isis might send an image of winged arms or appear as a great bird. Yemaya's song might invade your quiet contemplation. You may even receive insights when you're engaged in mundane tasks. You might be stirring a pot of spaghetti sauce on the stove, for instance, and suddenly feel Brigid beside you stirring her cauldron.

Pay attention to signs and synchronicities. If you see an animal or bird—especially one you might not ordinarily see in your usual setting—it could mean a deity is attempting to contact you. Many goddesses are associated with animals and birds: Aphrodite and Sophia with doves, Sekhmet and Tefnut with lions. Explore the symbolism associated with these creatures and with the goddesses to discover their meanings.

You can also petition a goddess through prayers, rituals, and other intentional actions. According to Buddhist thought, for example, lighting incense can invoke the spirit of the Buddha into a statue of him, and you could use this same practice to call upon the Asian goddess Kuan Yin. Earth goddesses may look kindly on you if you take care of the planet. Throughout this book I've suggested a variety of things you can do to solicit aid from the goddesses when you seek protection, healing, guidance, courage, abundance, or something else.

WORKING WITH THE GODDESSES

As you explore the myths and traditions of various cultures, you'll likely feel an affinity for certain goddesses who correspond to your heritage, vocation, or spiritual vision. For example, Scandinavians may relate to Freya, the Irish to Brigid, and the Japanese to Amaterasu. Artists may feel a kinship with Saraswati, whereas athletes may connect most to Nike. Some goddesses may be "right" for you at one period in your life, whereas others seem appropriate for your path at other stages of your development. Young women, for instance, might admire Artemis's vitality and independence. Older women may value the wisdom of Hecate or Sophia.

Whether you choose to honor a single goddess or many different deities is purely a personal choice. You may feel a strong connection to a particular goddess and think of her as your primary guide or patron. When you need a little extra help with a specific task, you can solicit the aid of a goddess whose attributes suit your need.

Are you going through a transition? Facing a challenge? Embarking on a new path? Do you want love, abundance, or creative inspiration? Whatever situation you're experiencing, whatever you seek, there's a goddess whose power can help you make the best of it. The appendices at the end of this book list the deities according to their attributes as well as the cultures that honored them.

MEET THE GODDESSES

In this book you will find seventy-five goddesses from around the world. Due to space constraints, the information shared here is only a portion of what these deities represent to the people who respect them and only covers some aspects of the goddesses' natures. You'll probably notice some of their stories overlap—the Mesopotamian goddess Ishtar, for example, bears many similarities to Sumer's Inanna. The ancient Romans subsumed many of the Greek deities into their pantheon, which is why I chose to write about the Greek goddesses and reference their Roman counterparts.

You'll also find that goddesses go by many names and honorary titles. Furthermore, their devotees tell a variety of legends about the deities. For instance, Kuan Yin is sometimes described as a goddess, sometimes as a bodhisattva and the female equivalent of the Buddha, and sometimes as a Chinese princess and Buddhist saint. These concepts are not firm and fixed. They change over time as cultures and thinking change. As the Shen Yun Performing Arts website explains, "Legends are like the shifting sands of a desert—forever changing, hard to grasp...and there are many versions." Although this can be confusing, it also shows the vast scope of the deities and the rich, evolving traditions that accompany them.

I urge you to continue reading about the goddesses included in this book to gain a greater understanding of their importance in humankind's history and how they still influence us today. I also hope you'll search for other goddesses as well that aren't mentioned in this book. Each has something to teach you. Each can open your eyes to a deeper knowledge of yourself and the world in which you live.

ADITI

"Aditi (Mother of the Universe, the Primal Being) is all the Heaven, Aditi is the space, Aditi is Mother, Father and Children. Aditi is all the Gods and Goddesses, Aditi is the five bases of creation. Aditi is all that has been and all that will take birth."
—Rig Veda 1.89.10

HISTORY AND MYTHOLOGY

In Sanskrit, the sky goddess Aditi's name means "limitless" or "boundless." Hindu mythology describes her as the feminine aspect of the supreme god Brahma. The ultimate creator goddess, she's responsible for having brought the entire cosmos into existence. The ancient texts known as the Vedas tell us she birthed the "spirits" of the zodiac, the planets, stars, and all the other celestial bodies, and she holds dominion over everything in the heavens. The personification of the sky, Aditi is the mother of all things in heaven and earth—both deities and mortals—including the gods Indra and Vishnu. One story says she's the mother of 330 million gods!

VIRTUES

Aditi the limitless enjoys complete freedom—nothing can contain or hinder her. People often call on her to release them from responsibilities and restrictions—from illnesses to debts to karmic conditions—so they may experience greater freedom.

Like the ever-changing sky (which she's said to hold up) and the planets that circle our sun, Aditi represents movement. She knows that nothing remains the same for long and the only constant is change. Nature's cycles, the phases of the moon, the ups and downs of human existence, the wheel of life, death, and rebirth are all part of Aditi's fluidity. Under her guidance, everything is in continual transition—energy cannot be destroyed, only transformed.

Because Aditi encompasses all, she's also considered a protector goddess. She oversees life on earth as well as the forces of the cosmos and governs their interaction. In her mother-goddess role, she safeguards humans and nurtures her devotees, and brings them abundance. Consequently, she's one of the most revered and beloved goddesses in India and other parts of Asia. Artists often depict this beautiful deity with several arms and seated on an open lotus blossom.

MANIFESTING HER POWER

Aditi can expand your perspective, enabling you to see the big picture. She shows you how to handle challenges by gaining greater insight and understanding. She teaches that everything is connected, and that although physical life on earth is temporal, the soul's life is eternal. Gaze up at the moon and stars and ask Aditi to let you experience yourself as part of the infinite cosmos. Once you realize that you are a spark of her limitless consciousness, you'll feel the freedom her truth offers.

Do you have a dream or goal that seems beyond your capabilities? Do you doubt yourself, thereby putting limits on what you can accomplish? Aditi teaches that you are more than what you believe yourself to be. Your possibilities are as limitless as the sky above. Light twelve candles in her honor (to represent the twelve solar months and the twelve signs in Vedic astrology) and request her assistance. Invite her to reveal your inner power and help you connect with it. Listen to her message: reach for the stars!

AINE

"Above all else, Aine was the people's Goddess, who gave much to them and received their love and worship in return."

—Judith Shaw, "Aine, Summer Goddess of Love, Light and Fertility," www.feminismandreligion.com

HISTORY AND MYTHOLOGY

The Celtic goddess Aine's name means many things, all of them good: bright, joy, splendor, radiance, and glory. She's linked with summertime and fruitfulness. According to legend, Aine created grain (literally birthed it) on the holiday known as Lammas or Lughnasadh and gave it to the Irish people.

Mythology tells us this benevolent shape-shifting goddess could turn herself into an exceptionally speedy red mare. She also rode horseback with her two sisters, Fennen and Grainne, under the full moon to visit the magical lake Lough Gur near her sacred hills, Cnoc Aine or Knockainy, in southwest Ireland. The lake was believed to hold healing powers, and Aine herself was revered as a healer deity. Myths connect Aine with water, and some say she was the daughter of the sea god Manannán mac Lir.

In her role as a goddess of love and fertility, Aine took mortal lovers and is said to have been mother to a race of faery-humans. Thus, she's also known as the Faery Queen. Legends say she married Gerald, the Earl of Desmond, and they had a son who became a powerful magician—perhaps he was even the great Merlin.

VIRTUES

As a protector goddess, Aine cared for the crops and animals. Because she was often linked with the sun and the moon, she was responsible for watching over the land and, by extension, the nourishment of all its inhabitants. In pre-Christian times—and even today—the Celts

celebrated her at Midsummer (the Summer Solstice) and at the harvest festival Lughnasad (also known as Lammas, on August 1).

One of the most beloved deities in the Celtic pantheon, Aine's powers include the ability to heal using hydrotherapy. In fact, legend says that the ill were often brought to her enchanted lake Lough Gur at Cnoc Aine, where the goddess treated their sickness. If she couldn't save their lives, she eased their passage into the Otherworld by singing their souls back home. Some stories say Aine now abides in the sacred lake.

Aine is often depicted with long red hair adorned by fallen stars. Sometimes she wears a yellow gown symbolizing the sun and moon or sometimes a green one to represent the earth's vegetation.

MANIFESTING HER POWER

Farmers, gardeners, and other people who work the land can petition this fertility goddess to make their plants grow strong and healthy. Consider planting some fresh herbs or a pretty rose bush to honor Aine. Even if you live in a city, you can grow herbs or flowers in containers. If you're interested in healing techniques that use botanicals, such as herbalism, flower remedies, or aromatherapy, ask Aine to reveal her secrets to you while you review common recipes for home remedies. Share what you learn with others to encourage their well-being.

Legend says Aine took human men as lovers in order to teach them the sacredness of love and sex. If you're seeking a deeper, more fulfilling love life or want to attract a partner who will engage you at a spiritual level as well as a sexual one, let Aine be your guide. Study the long-standing tradition of sacred and magical sex to infuse your relationship with greater meaning, passion, and love. You can find many books on the subject, including *Sex Magic for Beginners*.

AMATERASU

"Her gentle beauty and warmth radiated life force and hope throughout the blessed land of Japan, and far beyond. Amaterasu was the one who showed the people their beauty and potential."
—Melissa Osborne, "Amaterasu: Out of the Cave and Into the Light," www.lyricalworks.com

HISTORY AND MYTHOLOGY

The Japanese goddess of the sun, Amaterasu also holds such laudatory titles as Heaven Shining, Great August Deity, and Great Divinity Illuminating Heaven. As the most important goddess in the Shinto religion, she rules the sky as well as the region of the spirits known as *Takama no Hara*.

Mythology tells us she was born from the eye of her father, Izanagi, and her grandson, Jimmu, became Japan's first ruler. She had an annoying younger brother named Susano-O, the thunder god, who tormented her and caused her a great deal of trouble. According to a well-known legend, Susano-O killed a sacred horse and brought it to the weaving hall where Amaterasu was working with her sister. The incident upset the goddess so much that she withdrew into a cave, leaving the world without its sun goddess. The world plunged into darkness. Evil spirits rampaged through the land, unchecked by the goddess who ordinarily controlled them.

In an effort to draw her out of her isolation, other deities appealed to Amaterasu's love of beauty by positioning a tree decorated with jewels, gorgeous garments, and a mirror outside the cave. It wasn't until another goddess, Ama-no-Uzume, did a bawdy dance outside the cave and caused all the gods to laugh that Amaterasu peeked out to see what the fuss was about. One glimpse of her beautiful reflection in the mirror momentarily distracted Amaterasu, and the other dieties were able to grab her and bring her out of the cave.

In Japan, Shinto's most significant shrine at Ise is dedicated to Amaterasu. The mirror that is housed there is considered to be one of the three imperial treasures.

VIRTUES

This solar goddess's great beauty and generosity symbolize the sun's light, which animates life on earth. Amaterasu's dominion over the spirit realm suggests that light keeps darkness, evil spirits, and the underworld in check. She's also revered for having taught people how to grow rice and weave cloth. Therefore, she embodies the qualities of generosity, kindness, and creativity.

In Western psychology, the mirror that hung from the tree outside Amaterasu's cave represents recognizing what psychoanalyst Carl Jung called "the shadow," or the unacknowledged parts of ourselves, both loathsome and wondrous. In addition, the erotic dancing of the goddess Ama-no-Uzume may signify a connection with sexual energy and its creative power.

MANIFESTING HER POWER

Amaterasu urges you to see your own brilliance, for each of us shines with a unique radiance. If you feel unattractive or insignificant or unappreciated, call upon this goddess to help you identify your own value and express what's special about you. Dedicate a piece of jewelry, such as a necklace, to the goddess and wear it to attract her energy. You can also hang the necklace near your mirror to call in Amaterasu's presence.

Connecting with Amaterasu can help you face your inner shadow and bring it into the light. Is there a part of you that lies hidden that you are ashamed of? If so, ask the goddess to reveal it to you. Stand before your mirror and have an honest conversation with yourself: What do you accept about yourself? What don't you feel comfortable with? What would you like to understand more fully?

ANUKET

*"The Nile, forever new and old / Among the living and the dead /
Its mighty, mystic stream has rolled."*
—Henry Wadsworth Longfellow, *Christus, Part II: The Golden Legend*

HISTORY AND MYTHOLOGY

The people of ancient Egypt relied on the Nile River for their sustenance. Because of its power and importance, they also honored the goddess Anuket, the personification of the river. Said to be the daughter of the sun god Ra (or perhaps the water deities Khnum and Satis), Anuket governed the Nile's annual flooding, which brought fertility to the land and nurtured crops. Not surprisingly, she's also called the Giver of Life and is viewed as a goddess of abundance and prosperity. Some sources say her name means "to embrace" or "to surround," a reference to the land bordering the river.

Not only was Anuket worshipped in Egypt, she also reigned supreme in Nubia and the Sudan. Her main center of power is Elephantine Island, where the Nile begins its passage through Egypt. According to legend, people threw coins, jewelry, and other items of value into the Nile during Anuket's festival (when the river began its inundation) to thank the goddess and petition her for continued blessings. Traditionally, people ate fish during her celebration to honor her power.

VIRTUES

The goddess is often depicted with her arms arched over her head, in the shape of the crescent moon. Her arms symbolize the two tributaries that flow into the Nile. This posture also suggests she holds the Nile in her arms and/or that she draws down the moon into her embrace. Other images show her wearing a lavish headdress fashioned from feathers or reeds and holding an ankh, symbol of life. Sometimes she's nursing the pharaoh. Still other depictions give her a woman's body and the head of a gazelle, which connects her to the hunt (another sign of nourishment and bounty). Always, though, she represents life and fertility.

Anuket's festival, celebrated annually at the time when the Nile floods, points not only to fertility and prosperity, but also to the natural cycles and seasons that are part of life on earth. Therefore, the goddess represents the ongoing cycle of life, death, and rebirth.

MANIFESTING HER POWER

Like many water deities around the world, Anuket brings the blessings of abundance, fertility, and fulfillment. Seek her assistance in manifesting prosperity and happiness in your own life. What do you need to "water" to make your intentions grow and blossom? Perhaps you would like to deepen a relationship or expand your responsibilities at work. Toss a coin into a body of water to request Anuket's aid. Ask Anuket to help you adapt to the ups and downs that we all go through in our journey on earth.

In addition to the ebbs and flows we associate with water and with life, water also shows how patience and perseverance can wear down rocks and transform land over time. If you want to change a situation, but realize change must come slowly and naturally rather than through force, sit beside a body of water and allow it to calm you. Ask Anuket to guide you on her gently rolling currents as she would a mariner sailing down the Nile.

Anuket can also show you how to adapt to your personal life cycles. We all experience times of confidence and vitality, when we assert ourselves and act decisively in pursuit of our objectives. At other times, however, we feel a need to withdraw, regroup, and renew ourselves. Prepare and eat a meal of fish in Anuket's honor; she'll help you understand how to flow with your natural rhythms.

APHRODITE

"The force that unites the elements to become all things is Love, also called Aphrodite; Love brings together dissimilar elements into a unity, to become a composite thing."
—Empedocles, Greek philosopher

HISTORY AND MYTHOLOGY

Aphrodite is the goddess of love in ancient Greek mythology. Her counterpart in the Roman pantheon is Venus. One of the best-known and most beloved goddesses in the Western world, Aphrodite governs art, beauty, pleasure, feminine sexuality, and fertility.

Her birth, however, has a rather sordid side. According to one myth, she arose in adult form near Cyprus, emerging from sea foam resulting from the castration of her father, the sky-god Ouranos (Uranus), by his son Cronus. She washed ashore on a scallop shell, famously depicted in Botticelli's fifteenth-century painting *The Birth of Venus.* Homer's *Iliad,* however, claimed she was the daughter of Zeus and Dione.

Although married to the ugly and dour smith-god Hephaestus, she had an ongoing affair with her brother Ares (Mars in Roman myth). She's reputed to have engaged in affairs with other gods and mortals too, including the handsome Adonis. These relationships were inspired in part because of a magic girdle her husband fashioned for her that made her irresistible.

Many myths exist about Aphrodite. According to one well-known story, she entered into a divine beauty contest judged by the Trojan Paris, where she competed against the goddesses Athena and Hera. After Aphrodite bribed Paris by offering him the most desirable woman on earth, he awarded her the prize—a golden apple. But the deal had a downside. The woman Aphrodite offered Paris was the beautiful Helen of Troy, who happened to be married to the king of Sparta, and their affair led to the Trojan War.

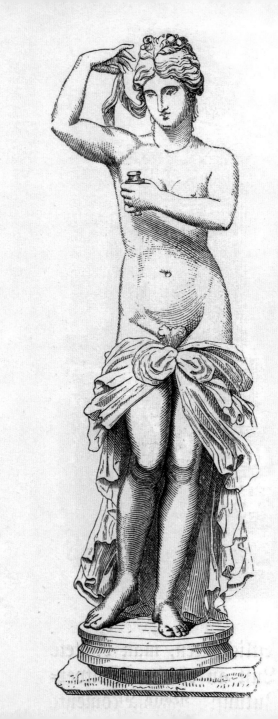

VIRTUES

The glamorous Aphrodite epitomizes our romantic ideals about love, relationships, sex, beauty, and pleasure. She represents joy and passion but shuns fidelity. The term *aphrodisiac* derives from her name, and according to legend, the beautiful goddess had the power to enchant anyone she pleased.

In ancient Greece, the priestesses who worshipped her engaged in the art of sacred sex to honor her power and bring blessings to the manifest world. As a fertility goddess, Aphrodite could influence the growth of crops as well as human procreation. Legend says she was a nurturing mother and encouraged her children in the arts, culture, and knowledge of all kinds.

Often Aphrodite is shown with a dove, her spirit companion and symbol of peace. However, the goddess was also known for her bad temper, vanity, and jealousy. She scorned those who didn't uphold her rites or who didn't show her enough veneration. One of these unfortunate fellows was the Greek prince Hippolytus, son of Theseus. Aphrodite caused his stepmother to fall in love with him, which ultimately led to his death.

MANIFESTING HER POWER

Call upon Aphrodite to help you attract a romantic partner or to rekindle the spark in an existing relationship. As the goddess of sexual love, she encourages you to explore your own sexuality and to express your sensual side in an unabashed manner. Read erotic poetry to get inspiration—or write your own.

Aphrodite can teach you to appreciate your unique beauty. Treat yourself to a facial or manicure and bask in the pleasure of your physicality. You may even want to experiment with a new hairstyle or cosmetics. Wear clothes that enhance your features and make you feel good about the way you look. Let Aphrodite help awaken your inner seductress. Attractiveness is more than physical beauty—show qualities such as sensuality, grace, sincerity, or adventurousness in relationships.

ARTEMIS

"Over the shadowy hills and windy peaks she draws her golden
bow….The tops of the high mountains tremble and
the tangled wood echoes awesomely with the outcry of beasts."

—Homer, *The Homeric Hymns*, "27–To Artemis"

HISTORY AND MYTHOLOGY

The Greeks' wild maiden goddess Artemis is echoed in Roman mythology as Diana. She's the daughter of the great god Zeus and his lover, Leto, and twin sister of the god Apollo. As a nature lover, Artemis lived in the forest among the animals and served as protector to both wild and domesticated creatures. Because of her connection to nature, some artists show her with a deer or other animal as a companion. However, Artemis is also known as the goddess of the hunt. According to legend, she hunted with the god Orion, whom she supposedly loved. Often she's depicted with a bow and quiver of arrows. Many legends about Artemis exist, and among the Olympians she's one of the most venerated goddesses.

Mythology tells us that the beautiful goddess rejected all lovers and asked her father to let her remain a virgin forever, free from the demands of a husband and family. When the Greek herdsman and hunter Aktaion observed her bathing nude, she angrily turned him into a stag and set his hounds upon him. The willful deity even insisted that the nymphs who accompanied her remain chaste. One legend says she killed the princess Ariadne because she'd been seduced by Theseus. In another story, Artemis shot and nearly killed her attendant Callisto because Zeus had impregnated her. (Hera, Zeus's wife, had turned Callisto into a bear for committing adultery with the god.)

VIRTUES

The proud, dynamic, and fiercely independent Artemis lived life on her own terms—and woe be to anyone who crossed her. As the legends about her show, she had a vindictive temperament and could be ruthless in exacting revenge. Usually she's depicted as a stern, serious deity whose only pleasures were hunting and nature. Although respected for her power and courage, she's often portrayed as cold, wrathful, and arrogant.

As a protector of nature, the goddess was responsible for both the wilderness and agriculture. Fertile fields, abundant crops, and healthy livestock were a sure sign that Artemis favored those who owned them. Blighted areas indicated the goddess's displeasure.

She's also considered a moon deity, linked specifically with the new and crescent phases associated with the maiden aspect of the Triple Goddess. Although Artemis rejected marriage and children of her own, she protects children and aids women during childbirth—she even assisted her own mother in the birth of Apollo.

MANIFESTING HER POWER

Artemis can help you become more independent and self-confident. She can also guide you as you learn to take risks, stand up to adversaries, and trust your own judgment. Devote some time each day to communicating with her in solitude, perhaps while taking a walk in a park or the woods. Bring a pretty stone or leaf home with you as a reminder that Artemis is available to assist you.

If you're the outdoorsy type or plan on spending time in nature, ask Artemis to accompany you. Whether you're hiking in the mountains or whitewater rafting, she can keep you safe and ensure you have a good time. To win her favor, donate to environmental groups or animal protection organizations.

Ask Artemis to help you win an athletic event or excel at your favorite sport. She's the perfect patron to inspire a girls' team. Honor her by drawing or embroidering an arrow on your athletic gear.

ATHENA

"As an archetype, Athena is the pattern followed by logical women, who are ruled by their heads rather than their hearts."

—Jean Shinoda Bolen, MD, *Goddesses in Everywoman*

HISTORY AND MYTHOLOGY

This Greek goddess (whose Roman counterpart is Minerva) had a most unusual birth: she emerged fully grown from the head of the great god Zeus and had no mother. Some accounts say Athena was born wearing armor. However, this warrior goddess took no pleasure in battle; she used her powers to defend the state against outside aggression, and, as such, became respected as a true patriot by her people. According to some legends, Athena was her father's favorite child and the only one he trusted with his fabled weapon, the thunderbolt.

Athena is honored as the goddess of wisdom, reason, literature, art, and other intellectual pursuits—perhaps due to the conditions of her birth. She's also considered a virgin deity, more concerned with the mind than the body—an independent goddess who bowed to no god or man.

Mythology tells us Athena became the goddess of the city of Athens after winning a contest with Poseidon. Both deities gave the people of Athens a gift: Poseidon a salt spring and Athena an olive tree. The people chose Athena's gift, and the olive tree remains an important source of food and revenue for Greece to this day. She also plays a role in many myths, including guiding Perseus in his quest to slay the monstrous Gorgon Medusa and directing Jason as he built his ship, the *Argo*, to search for the fabled Golden Fleece. In Homer's epic, the *Odyssey*, she encourages Telemachus to find his father, Odysseus.

Many temples were built to honor Athena, including the Parthenon on the Acropolis in Athens. There is also a smaller temple nearby that is

known as the Temple of Athena Nike, *nike* being a Greek term that translates as "victory."

VIRTUES

Best known for her intellectual prowess, Athena is often depicted with an owl, the symbol of wisdom, as her companion. She wears a helmet and carries a spear and a shield. She is the only Olympian goddess who appears dressed in armor. She was an unparalleled strategist in battle, practical and prudent, as well as a divine protector.

According to legend, the innovative Athena introduced many useful inventions into the world, including the ship, chariot, yoke and plow, bridle, trumpet, and flute. A patron of craftspeople, she's also credited with teaching mortals pottery and weaving. She's respected for her ethical character and for her diligence in maintaining the state's structure, industry, and prosperity. Athena applied her intelligence and reason to promote law, order, and justice in the courts and in society.

MANIFESTING HER POWER

As goddess of the intellect, Athena can aid you in any mental endeavor. Call upon her to assist you if you want to ace an exam, learn a new subject or skill, or gain insight into a perplexing matter. Display an image of an owl in a prominent place to signal your desire for wisdom and Athena's blessing. She can also spark your ingenuity and show you how to be more inventive in handling problems. Olives, which she gave to Athens, are considered a "brain-healthy" food, so cook with olive oil to nourish your gray matter.

If you're facing a challenge or feel threatened by an adversary, ask Athena to give you the courage and clarity to see the way out of your dilemma. Make her picture your cellphone's home screen or print a picture and carry it with you to sense her presence. As you listen to her wise counsel, you may hear her advising you to use intellect and ingenuity rather than force.

BADB

HISTORY AND MYTHOLOGY

A war goddess in Celtic mythology, Badb is often linked with the Morrigan, the Irish goddess of death. Badb is sometimes described as one of the Morrigan's sisters who make up a trio of deities known as the Morrigan. Like the Morrigan and two other war goddesses, Nemain and Macha, Badb was a shape-shifter who turned herself into a hooded crow (or a raven) and flew above battlefields, squawking to confuse and terrify the warriors fighting below. Her name means "fury," and battlefields were often known as "the land of Badb."

According to some stories, these sisters were also sisters to three goddesses of the land: Eriu, Fotla, and Banba. In addition to showing herself as a crow, Badb is also associated with horses. Because of this, she has ties to the Celtic horse goddesses Rhiannon and Epona.

Ancient Celtic women were known to fight alongside their men in battle. This could explain why we find Badb and other female deities overseeing war. Badb herself, however, did not actually engage in the fight—her role was to generate frenzy and chaos among the soldiers. Legend says she gloried in the carnage of war. At night, after the fighting ended, the goddess reputedly gathered up the heads of the dead.

Mythology connects Badb with the Tuatha Dé Danann, a race of Irish deities who descended from the goddess Danu and later became the faery people of Ireland. She's said to have helped them win the second battle at *Mag Tuireadh* in Ireland and gain their freedom from the Formorians.

VIRTUES

Legend considers Badb a prophet who could foresee the future. Like the Morrigan (and the Irish *bean sidhe* or banshee), Badb predicted death by shrieking hideously. She's thought of as a goddess of witches, sorcery, and magic. In fact, she used her magic powers to determine who would die in battle and which side would win the war.

Some sources say she had blue or blood-red lips. Sometimes she took the form of a miniature female as she flew through the sky. On other occasions, she appeared as a beautiful young woman, a hag, or a giant. When taking the form of a giant, Badb helped soldiers across rivers. She's also said to have shape-shifted into a wolf or a bear when it suited her purposes.

MANIFESTING HER POWER

This fierce goddess of war can guide you when you're facing a frightening challenge. Whether you're fighting in an actual battle, confronting an adversary on the playing field, or encountering opposition in your workplace, try to channel Badb's courage and determination. She can also show you how to confuse your enemy and create a chaotic situation, thus allowing you to win the conflict. To solicit her favor, feed crows (they like peanuts).

Badb's magical skill and ability to predict the future can help you tap into your own "second sight." With expanded vision, you can see what lies ahead and avoid pitfalls, accidents, or mistakes. Light a candle to Badb and gaze into the flame to see images of things to come. Start paying close attention to your intuition and notice when you receive insight or warnings—"coincidences" may be communications from the goddess.

BAST

"Bastet invites us in for snuggling comfort in the Lap of Joy."
—Nancy Blair, *Goddesses for Every Season*

HISTORY AND MYTHOLOGY

Also known as Bastet, this cat goddess was one of ancient Egypt's favorite deities, and she remains popular with Wiccans and pagans today. Originally she had the head of a lioness, but later depictions show her as a domestic cat. Cats were considered sacred in Egypt, and Bast's priests and priestesses kept cats in temples dedicated to the goddess.

Because cats killed rodents, thereby protecting crops and preventing diseases, Bast became known as a protector deity and was called the "Eye of Ra." Paintings show early Egyptians hunting with cats, and when a prominent person died, his or her cats were mummified and entombed too, so they could accompany the deceased into the afterlife. One funeral temple in lower Egypt contained 300,000 feline mummies!

Bast's lineage can get a bit fuzzy, however, she's generally thought of as the daughter of the sun god Ra and the wife of Ptah (who was also married to the lion-headed goddess Sekhmet). She had two sons, the lion god Mahes (Mihos) and Nefertum, god of aromatherapy.

Although Bast was a huntress and behaved fiercely at times, she's best known for her playful, pleasure-loving nature. Her festival, Bubastis, involved plenty of drinking, feasting, music, dancing, sensuality, and merrymaking of all kinds.

VIRTUES

This fun-loving goddess teaches us the benefits of play and urges us to do what pleases us. Our word *pleasure* comes from one of her names, Pasht. She's associated with grace, beauty, art, sexuality, and creature comforts. Because Bast loved music and dancing, paintings often depict her holding a *sistrum*, a type of rattle played at her festivals.

Sometimes Bast carries an ankh, symbol of life, and/or a papyrus wand, which stood for Lower Egypt, where the goddess reigned. Statues show her wearing a *wesekh* or *menat*, a collar-type necklace popular with Egyptian deities and mortals alike, and earrings to signify her fondness for beautiful things.

The hieroglyph for Bast is the same as the one marked on bas jars, which held expensive perfumes. The Egyptians prized these aromatics for both their seductive properties and their medicinal ones; thus we see the links to the goddess's protective powers and her sensuality. As a fertility goddess, she's sometimes shown with a litter of kittens that she lovingly nurtures.

MANIFESTING HER POWER

The early Egyptians displayed statues of Bast in their homes for protection against robbers. You may want to do the same. Place an image of the goddess near your front door as a divine guardian.

Bast can teach you how to have more fun and enjoy life more fully. She understands that all work and no play makes for a dull existence. If you share your home with a feline friend, dedicate some time each day to playing with your companion. You can even view funny videos of cats online or volunteer at an animal shelter, especially during spring when you can watch kittens and their antics.

Let Bast help you appreciate sensuality and pleasure. Find a comfortable spot to relax and bask in the sunshine with your favorite food or beverage. Play music and dance, trying to imitate the cat goddess's fluid grace.

BRANWEN

"Our task must be to free ourselves from this prison by widening our circle of compassion to embrace all living creatures and the whole of nature in its beauty."
—Albert Einstein

HISTORY AND MYTHOLOGY

This Welsh/Celtic goddess of love and beauty is the daughter of the sea god Llyr and Penarddun, sister of Bran the Blessed, and wife of the Irish king Matholuch. Her name means "white raven." Mythology considers her one of a trio of goddesses of Avalon (along with Cerridwen and Arianrhod), the youthful or maiden aspect of the Triple Goddess. Legend links her with a sacred mountain in Wales, Cadair Bronwen, which means "Branwen's Seat."

According to myth, King Matholuch and the beautiful Branwen fell in love, and although it was unheard of for a woman of her clan to marry a foreigner, her family allowed the wedding to take place anyway. It was known that Branwen would bear the next king of Wales, and Matholuch hoped their son would also rule Ireland. However, Branwen's brother, Evnissyen, disapproved of the match and, in a rage, injured the Irishmen's horses. As compensation, Bran the Blessed gave Matholuch a magic cauldron that would bring any soldier killed in battle back to life.

Unsatisfied with the deal and seeking revenge, the Irish demanded Branwen be punished. For three years she slaved in a kitchen, where she was beaten and humiliated. When Bran the Blessed heard about her plight, he retaliated by bringing a Welsh army to Ireland. Despite Branwen's pleas for peace, a war broke out between the two nations. The Irish put their dead warriors in the cauldron and resurrected them. Bran the Blessed was slain, and Branwen, devastated that so many had been killed over her, died of a broken heart.

Some sources say Branwen's sad story represents the end of matriarchal culture and the rise of patriarchy.

VIRTUES

Even though the Irish treated Branwen badly, the goddess tried to keep her own people from retaliating. This desire and her patient forbearance during her years of enslavement show her kind and peaceful nature, and her ability to forgive. Her courage and compassion serve as inspiration for those who must bear harsh situations or who are treated unfairly. Legend says the goddess frees abused wives from their cruel husbands and helps them begin new, happier lives.

Sometimes depicted as a raven-haired beauty, sometimes as a friend to ravens and sparrows, the goddess was incapable of hate or vengeance. She could only express love—and love and grief ultimately cost Branwen her life. The magic cauldron symbolizes the womb and fertility. Witches and wizards consider it a feminine tool in their spell practice.

MANIFESTING HER POWER

If you feel you're being treated unjustly, ask Branwen to lend you the strength to endure the situation until you can find a way out of it. Women who are in unhappy or abusive relationships can call upon Branwen for aid. She can teach you to marshal your inner strength and give you the clarity to set boundaries or break free from the unhealthy situation. Invite Branwen to go for a walk with you. As you keep putting one foot ahead of the other, feel the goddess helping you grow stronger, step by step, through adversity.

Has someone wronged you? This goddess of love can show you how to find forgiveness in your heart, instead of seeking revenge or holding a grudge. Write a letter of forgiveness and burn it in a cauldron to release hard feelings that could otherwise fester and prevent you from being at peace.

BRIGID

*"Brigid is the all-provider, the nurturer, enabling
the Spirit to survive in bodily form."*
—Shirley Toulson, *The Celtic Year*

HISTORY AND MYTHOLOGY

This beloved goddess is a favorite of the Irish people and one of the most powerful deities in the Celtic pantheon. Her name means "exalted one." Mythology tells us Brigid was the daughter of Ireland's great god Dagda. She married Bres, a king from a hostile tribe, and together they had three sons who became great warriors. When Christianity moved into Ireland, the Catholic Church adopted the goddess and canonized her as Saint Brigid.

Brigid goes by many names, including Lady of the Flame, Goddess of the Hearth, Bright One, and Breo-saighead, meaning "fiery arrow." She has three rivers named for her—Brigit in Ireland, Braint in Wales, and Brent in England—as well as many wells and springs. At the most famous of her shrines near Kildare, where a great oak revered by the Druids grew, priestesses learned healing, poetry, music, divination, and other knowledge. They also cared for Brigid's sacred wells and groves, and kept a fire burning constantly.

In pagan tradition, the holiday Imbolc is dedicated to Brigid. Also known as Candlemas, it is usually celebrated from the evening of January 31 until February 2. At this time in the Northern Hemisphere, the days are growing longer and, although winter still holds the land in a frozen grip, Imbolc heralds the promise of spring. Imbolc means "in the belly," and the holiday honors all forms of creativity—of the mind as well as the body.

VIRTUES

The goddess of healing, smithcraft, and poetry, Brigid presides over both the homemaker's cook fire and the metal smith's forge. At first glance, she seems a contradiction. As a solar goddess, she offers the fiery gifts of light (knowledge), inspiration (associated with the fire element), and the healing vitality of the sun. Yet she also has connections with water, signifying intuition and the power of divination. Thus, she represents a blend of feminine and masculine energies, body and mind, and the union of polarities necessary for creation.

Illustrations of Brigid sometimes show her stirring a great cauldron, the witch's magic tool that symbolizes the womb and the receptive, fertile nature of the Divine Feminine. As goddess of inspiration, Brigid encourages everyone, regardless of gender, to stir the inner cauldron of creativity that exists within.

MANIFESTING HER POWER

Creative people, especially poets and musicians, can call upon Brigid to spark inspiration. Light candles in her honor and thank her for her assistance. Gaze at the flickering flames to focus your attention as you allow your imagination to expand.

Women who wish to become pregnant may connect with the fertile nature of this goddess. Legend says that Brigid protects all life under her green mantle. A patron of children and midwives, she attends every birth. According to an old fertility ritual, you can build a small fire in a magic cauldron dedicated to Brigid and jump over it to encourage pregnancy.

Healers and those who seek healing may petition Brigid for aid. Take a ritual bath by candlelight to gain insight and guidance from the goddess, or write your request on a piece of paper. Build a small fire in a cauldron and drop the paper in the flame while you envision your wish coming true.

CERRIDWEN

"The tag which Gwion and Ceridwen play is a common pursuit
on a shamanic journey, where, in the shape of his animal
the shaman pursues other animals through the otherworlds
in order to gain power or knowledge for another."
—Caitlin and John Matthews, *The Encyclopedia of Celtic Wisdom*

HISTORY AND MYTHOLOGY

This Celtic mother goddess's name comes from the word *cerru*, mean-ing "cauldron," a symbol of fertility. Cerridwen's legend begins with her marriage to a man named Tegid Voel. Together, she and Tegid had three children: Creirwy, Morvran, and Taliesin. (Some sources say they had a fourth, named Avagddu.) According to mythology, Morvran was hideously ugly, so Cerridwen decided to concoct a magic herbal brew that would make him wise. She left a boy named Gwion Bach in charge of stirring the potion in her cauldron of inspiration for one year and a day. Gwion, how-ever, accidentally spilled three drops on his finger and stuck his burned finger in his mouth. In that instant, he unwittingly gained magical know-ledge, but the rest of the potion turned to poison.

Afraid that Cerridwen would be angry with him, Gwion shape-shifted into a hare to hide, but the goddess wasn't fooled. She in turn shape-shifted into a greyhound and pursued him. Gwion tried to escape by shifting into a fish, but Cerridwen transformed into an otter. When he changed into a bird, she became a hawk. In desperation, Gwion took the form of a kernel of corn. Cerridwen shape-shifted into a hen and ate him. The magic grain grew inside her and was reborn as her son. The irate Cerridwen planned to kill the baby (the reincarnation of Gwion), but couldn't bring herself to do it. Instead, she put him in a leather bag and dumped him into the sea. Legend has it that the boy was rescued and grew up to be the famous Welsh bard, Taliesin.

VIRTUES

The cauldron is a magical tool for witches who consider Cerridwen their beloved patron. She is revered as a fertility goddess, for the cauldron, shaped like the womb, symbolizes fertility, nurturance, inspiration, and creativity. In her role as mother, she demonstrates she was both cruel and compassionate.

The wise Cerridwen is a skilled herbalist and enchantress who knows the secrets of the plant world and how to mix up a powerful magic potion. Her most notable characteristic, however, is her ability to transform herself into various creatures in order to accomplish her objectives. As a shape-shifter, she represents the shamanic power to journey through the realms of earth, air, and water. Her transformations also signify the ongoing cycle of life, death, and rebirth.

MANIFESTING HER POWER

Are you required to play a number of roles in life? The shape-shifting Cerridwen can teach you how to change your image to present yourself in different ways to different people. Take some time to read about spirit animals and identify which ones have qualities you admire. Seek Cerridwen's assistance in developing those qualities so you can "shape-shift" as needed.

If you're interested in learning the art of green or natural magic, ask Cerridwen to share her secrets with you. She'll show you how to use botanicals to heal, protect, and enchant. Acquire a small cauldron and practice concocting magic brews. Cerridwen can assist you in preparing plant-based remedies for all sorts of medicinal purposes.

CHANG'E

"An ancient legend says a beautiful Chinese girl called Chang-O has been living there for 4,000 years. It seems she was banished to the Moon because she stole the pill of immortality from her husband. You might also look for her companion, a large Chinese rabbit."

—*Apollo 11* flight journal, on the day of the 1969 moon landing

HISTORY AND MYTHOLOGY

The Chinese Moon Goddess, Chang'e (or Chang-O), once worked for the Jade Emperor, who was the ruler of heaven, but when she accidentally broke a precious vase of his, he exiled her to earth. On earth as a peasant girl, Chang'e befriended an archer named Hou Yi. One morning, to everyone's surprise, ten suns rose in the sky instead of one (some sources say they were the children of the Jade Emperor) and began burning the land. The marksman Hou Yi shot down nine of the suns, saving the world and therefore gaining fame and honor. Soon after Hou Yi became king and he married his beloved moon goddess, Chang'e.

After becoming king, Hou Yi arranged to have a magic potion formulated so he would become immortal. However, somehow Chang'e swallowed it first (legends differ on why), and it caused her to float up to the moon. She lived there for the rest of her existence, along with her friend the Jade Rabbit, known for his skills as an herbalist. Some sources say Chang'e only drank half of the elixir and Hou Yi drank the other half. He then rose into the sky and settled on the sun. The two deities represent the universal forces of yin (feminine) and yang (masculine).

VIRTUES

The Chinese celebrate the festival of Chang'e on the fifteenth day of the eighth month, according to the Chinese lunar calendar (in late

September or early October). This full moon harvest festival is one of the most important of the year—a time to give thanks for the earth's bounty. Women often petition the goddess for blessings and other participants feast under the full moon.

Like other moon goddesses, Chang'e is linked with fertility and women's health and well-being. As a harvest deity, she governs the fruitfulness of the land—her husband's salvation of the earth from the ten scorching suns echoes this power.

The legend of Chang'e also describes love and immortality. Some stories emphasize the devotion between her and Hou Yi. Some speak of her sadness at being separated from her husband, and others say she drank all the elixir of immortality and he was furious with her. The many versions of the myth represent the intricacies of marriage as well as the complementary energies, yin and yang, that create wholeness.

MANIFESTING HER POWER

Request good fortune from the moon goddess Chang'e. She can help you attract abundance of all kinds. Let her show you how to reap a bountiful harvest in your life and bring your dreams to fruition. On the day of her festival, make rice cakes, round like the full moon, and eat them in her honor.

Ask Chang'e to guide you in balancing the yin and yang forces in your life. Regardless of gender, we all have both feminine and masculine energies in us, and we must learn to integrate them in order to achieve harmony. Display a yin-yang symbol in a place where you'll see it often to remind you of your intention.

CHANGING WOMAN

"In the depth of winter, I finally learned that within me there lay an invincible summer."
—Albert Camus, French philosopher

HISTORY AND MYTHOLOGY

Also known as Asdzáá nádleehé, Changing Woman personifies the earth in Navajo mythology. The Apache call her Estsanatlehi or White Painted Woman. As her name indicates, she's always changing. In springtime she appears as a beautiful young woman, and in winter she's an elder. She never dies but continually renews herself. One legend tells us Changing Woman's birth brought order out of chaos and resulted in the Fourth World, where we live today.

When she came of age, she took the sun as her spouse and gave birth to twin boys. After only eight (some sources say twelve) days, the twins had reached maturity and began fighting the evil monsters and giants who roamed the earth, using magic weapons their father had given them. When they had destroyed all but four monsters, Changing Woman created the first human beings. According to one story, she formed their bodies from white flour and cornmeal that she brought forth from her breasts. Another says the goddess scraped off some of her skin and used it to fashion the people who became the Navajo.

Pleased with her work, Changing Woman gave the mortals her blessing and traveled across a rainbow to her turquoise castle that floats on the water in the west. There the sun, her consort, comes to her in the evenings. Like other earth goddesses, Changing Woman continues to provide for her people. It's said she allowed the four monsters not killed by her sons to remain on earth, however, so that human beings wouldn't become too complacent and would value what the goddess gave them. These monsters still live among us today: poverty, old age, winter, and famine.

VIRTUES

Goddess of the earth, Changing Woman, has dominion over nature, the plants and animals, as well as the humans who live on the planet. She represents the changing seasons and the stages of life. Her changing image, from youth to old age and back to youth again, symbolizes the cycle of the year. Therefore, Changing Woman also signifies renewal and rebirth.

As a mother-creator deity, she has the power to generate life. She governs reproduction and the fertility of humans as well as the earth. Described as a benevolent, loving goddess, she takes care of her people and protects them. From her body she brings forth all the necessities for life.

Her cycles are celebrated in Navajo ceremonies that mark childbirth, puberty, marriage, and the establishment of a new home. At these ceremonies, the people sing songs to honor the goddess.

MANIFESTING HER POWER

After a time of stress or trauma, ask Changing Woman to help you revitalize yourself. She'll show you ways to renew your mind, body, and spirit. Turquoise is often considered a healing stone, and legend says it's a favorite of the goddess. Wear turquoise jewelry to attract her aid and encourage your own healing.

Call upon Changing Woman to join you in honoring important passages and cycles in your life. She reminds you that you're not the same person today that you were yesterday, nor the one you will be tomorrow. At the change of each season, decorate your home with objects from nature to connect you with the Wheel of the Year, the annual cycle of seasons and the eight major holidays celebrated by pagans.

COATLICUE

"The boundaries which divide Life from Death are at best shadowy and vague. Who shall say where the one ends, and the other begins?"

—Edgar Allan Poe, "The Premature Burial"

HISTORY AND MYTHOLOGY

One of the most important Aztec deities, the goddess Coatlicue was responsible for maintaining the planet and everything on it. She's also known as Teteoinan, or "Mother of the Gods." In mythology, she's a personification of the feminine force, a complex goddess of both life and death.

The Aztecs also credited Coatlicue with having created the heavenly bodies. She's the mother of Huitzilopochtli, god of the sun and war; the moon goddess Coyolxauhqui; and 400 children collectively called the Huiztnaua, who were the stars. Some sources say she also birthed humankind. According to one legend, the Huiztnaua planned to attack and murder their mother, but Huitzilopochtli stopped them. He supposedly killed his siblings, including his sister Coyolxauhqui, whose head he chopped off and flung into the sky to create the moon. The story may symbolize the day's power over night or perhaps a shift from a lunar to a solar calendar and a change from matriarchal culture to a patriarchal one.

The most famous statue of Coatlicue, discovered in 1790, stands ten feet high and shows the deity headless, wearing a necklace of human body parts and a skirt made of snakes—her name means "serpent skirt." The basalt monolith is now housed in Mexico City's National Museum of Anthropology.

VIRTUES

Usually Coatlicue appears as a fierce older woman who has borne many children. As such, she's known for protecting women and their infants during childbirth. She is quite terrifying as both a creator and a destroyer deity who, like the earth itself, gives and takes away life. She is often depicted wearing a gory necklace made of human hands, hearts, and skulls, which may symbolize the earth as a devouring mother who ultimately kills all her offspring. However, another more positive interpretation explains that the goddess holds the remains of her children to her breast in order to purify and regenerate them.

Coatlicue is also the goddess of agriculture, responsible for the earth's fruitfulness. The Aztecs worshipped her at celebrations held during the rainy spring planting season and in the fall at harvest time.

MANIFESTING HER POWER

If you or someone you know will give birth soon, invite Coatlicue to protect mother and child during the process. The goddess has brought forth hundreds of children of her own, including the sun, moon, and stars. Her frightening appearance can scare away harmful energies and support a safe delivery. Acquire an image of a snake—if possible, one engraved on a stone—and give it to the prospective mother as a talisman. The snake symbolizes wisdom, power, sexuality, and transformation.

As a creator-destroyer goddess who presides over both life and death, Coatlicue can assist you through a transformative process. Is there some part of you that must die so that something else can be born? Perhaps you need to be fierce in destroying an old habit or unwanted behavior that's standing in the way of your growth. Ask Coatlicue to help you let go of the old and welcome the new. You may want to acquire a small representation of a skull, perhaps made of quartz crystal or another gemstone you like. Display it in a place where you'll see it often to remind yourself of your intention.

DANU

"Danu is everywhere, she is in every living thing, and like a good mother, she stands firm, giving of her love and support. Danu allows us our mistakes, never forcing decisions or actions. Yet when we are in our greatest need, she bends down to offer a comforting hand."

—Michelle Skye, *Goddess Alive!*

HISTORY AND MYTHOLOGY

Said to be the oldest of the Celtic deities, Danu harkens back to ancient matriarchal cultures and earth-based spirituality. She's the founder of the fabled race of Irish deities known as the Tuatha Dé Danann—which means the "people of Danu"—and is believed to be the mother of its leader, Dagda (although some stories say she was his mate or daughter). According to mythology, the Tuatha Dé Danann were living in exile when the goddess found them and, in the form of a cloud, returned them to their homeland. In her role as a creator-fertility goddess, she taught them agriculture, and under her gentle guidance, they became the wisdom bearers, the healers, the bards, and the Druids.

Her name's root, *dan*, translates as "wisdom," "abundance/wealth," "skill," and "art," and she's considered the Mother of Ireland. Danu also means "flowing one," and she's connected with rivers, streams, and wells, but her influence isn't limited to Ireland—Europe's great Danube River is named for her.

VIRTUES

All early agrarian, goddess-based cultures honor one or more fertility deities. In Celtic mythology, the primary mother goddess is Danu. Her fertile nature links her with both the land and water—and indeed, both are necessary for the growth of crops and to support life in general.

Her moniker the "flowing one" and her association with moving water symbolizes the importance of living in harmony with the passage of time, honoring the seasons of our lives, and growing through the ebbs and flows we encounter during our journey on planet earth. In this capacity, Danu brings the power to wash away blockages and impurities in order to restore clarity and balance, not by force, but through gentle persistence.

Legends also connect Danu in her land-goddess aspect with Ireland's holy stones and sites, such as Newgrange. She's said to visit the *sidhe*, burrows or hills believed to be the homes of the faery folk (as well as portals into other realms of existence). Some myths say the Tuatha Dé Danann retreated from the world we know into the magical land of faery and still reside there today.

MANIFESTING HER POWER

Like all mother-fertility goddesses, Danu can offer support and guidance to those who are about to become parents (or who already have children to nurture and protect). In her role as a fertility deity, she can aid anyone who is birthing a child of the mind or of the body. She can also lend her wisdom and strength to women who serve as matriarchs of a clan/family and help them steer the course through changing times with grace. Choose a special stone—ammonite, if possible—to link you with the sacred stones in Danu's homeland and to her strength and wisdom. Hold the stone while you sit beside a body of water and sense the goddess's protection.

As the "flowing one," Danu can guide you through the ebbs and flows of your ever-evolving life. Mark the pagan holidays (the Wheel of the Year) in order to attune yourself with ancient rhythms, the seasons of the year, and to discover your deep-seated affinity with all of nature.

DEMETER

"In all emerging agricultural societies, kneading dough and baking bread were acts symbolic of fertility. Made of grain—the sacred gift of agriculture—bread baked by a mother for her family combined earth, hearth, and love."

—Leonard Shlain, *The Alphabet versus the Goddess*

HISTORY AND MYTHOLOGY

Known as the goddess who made everything grow, Demeter obviously holds an important position in Greek mythology. Some sources say she even predates ancient Greece and associate her with Mother Earth or Gaia. She's sometimes called the Goddess of Grain or the Corn Goddess—the name of her Roman counterpart, Ceres, is the root of our word *cereal*. The daughter of Cronus and his sister Rhea, Demeter was swallowed at birth by her father (as were four of her siblings). However, eventually Cronus vomited up his children after Rhea tricked him into eating a stone.

In one myth, Demeter's brother Zeus raped and impregnated her with their daughter, Persephone (a.k.a., Kore). One day while Persephone was picking flowers, Zeus's brother Hades abducted the girl and took her to the underworld to be his wife, all with Zeus's permission. For nine days, the devastated Demeter searched for her only child. On the tenth day, the goddess Hecate accompanied her to seek help from the sun god Helios. When he refused, Demeter left Olympia to live among the mortals.

The grieving mother turned her back on the world and refused to make anything grow on earth until her daughter returned. When the extinction of the human race seemed likely, Zeus sent the messenger god Hermes to the underworld to convince Hades to free Persephone. Before he allowed the girl to leave, however, Hades gave her some pomegranate seeds to eat. Hermes brought the girl back to Demeter, but because

Persephone had eaten the seeds, she was doomed to spend part of each year with Hades. The time when Persephone resides in the underworld coincides with the barren winter season.

VIRTUES

Gentle Demeter epitomizes the devoted mother. Her role as goddess of agriculture also shows her fertile nature, for she nurtures the crops and controls the harvest. Thus, she cares for all humankind as her "children." Often she's depicted as a golden-haired matron, holding a sheaf of wheat or sometimes a cornucopia. As the myth of Demeter and Persephone describes, she also governs the seasons. Some mythologists suggest Demeter and Persephone are actually two aspects of the same goddess: mother and maiden.

Although Demeter is usually represented as a kind, generous, and helpful deity whom the gods treat badly, she shows her strength and determination when her child is kidnapped.

Demeter (along with Persephone) not only governs the cycle of seasons but she also represents the cycle of life, death, and rebirth. For 2,000 years she was celebrated at Greece's sacred and secret Eleusinian Mysteries.

MANIFESTING HER POWER

Demeter can help you identify your maternal and nurturing side. Her passionate spirit can help you care for your family and friends with kindness and devotion. Let her guide you through the challenges of raising children, forming friendships, and maintaining family bonds. Invite the goddess to join you when you prepare meals, and ask her to help you greet the world with kindness. Thank her by donating to a food bank or charity.

Ask the goddess to heal your inner child. In meditation, seek out the wounded, vulnerable part of yourself. This might be time to admit something you are ashamed of, or relive an emotionally draining memory. Feel Demeter holding you in her loving embrace each time you eat a food made from grain. Allow her to nurture you with her regenerative spirit.

DURGA

"I am the Queen, the gatherer-up of treasures, most
thoughtful, first of those who merit worship."
—Rig Veda 10.125.3

HISTORY AND MYTHOLOGY

In Hindu mythology Durga is considered the Mother of the Universe,
the first goddess. She creates, maintains, and destroys everything in
the world. One ancient text describes her as the Supreme Being. Her
name translates from Sanskrit as "fort" or "something unassailable." It
also means "one who eliminates suffering." Therefore, the indestruc-
tible Durga protects her earthly children and eases the pain of human
existence.

Sometimes she's described as the wife of Shiva and mother of the
deities Lakshmi, Saraswati, Ganesh, and Kartikeya. This complex goddess has many manifestations and many names, including Shakti, which
can confuse Westerners. Ultimately, all Hindu goddesses are different
aspects of the Goddess (or Devi).

Mythology also shows the beautiful Durga as a warrior goddess, willing to battle evil forces that threaten her creations or what's good and
right and sacred. One legend says the gods came together and combined
their energy to produce Durga, who turned out to be more powerful than
all the other deities. Riding on the back of a lion (or a tiger), she fought
a monstrous demon and prevented him from destroying everything in
heaven and earth. (This story is also told of Kali.) The lion on which Durga
rides can be seen as a symbol of pride as well as strength and leadership. Her commanding position signifies the power that results from
taming the inner beast. Therefore, the "battle" may be interpreted as a
struggle against the ego.

VIRTUES

Artists usually show Durga with either eight or ten arms (sometimes more) that represent Hinduism's eight (or ten) directions. With these the goddess protects and guides everything, everywhere. In her hands she holds objects that symbolize her creative and destructive powers: a conch shell, a bow and arrow, a thunderbolt, a lotus flower, a discus, a sword, and a trident. These symbols not only represent the weapons Durga uses to protect her devotees but they also suggest the "tools" needed to overcome ego and follow the spiritual life.

The goddess has three eyes—the left signifies the moon, the right corresponds to the sun, and the center represents knowledge. Often she wears golden-yellow or red to indicate her connection to the fire element. Some sources link her with Mother Nature. Revered for her creative power, courage, and intelligence, Durga is worshipped in India, Nepal, and other parts of Asia.

MANIFESTING HER POWER

Seen as the most powerful of all deities and the source of everything, this awe-inspiring mother goddess encourages you to honor and express the feminine force in the universe and in yourself (whether you're a woman or a man). Durga's creative energy can inspire and intensify your own fruitfulness. Call on her to help you fulfill your potential, produce wondrous works of art, or birth new ideas. Light golden-yellow candles in her honor, to thank her for her assistance.

Durga can guide you as you fight the good fight. Ask her to lend you her formidable energy and wisdom so you can stand up for what's right. She'll help you defeat the demons around or within you and emerge victorious. Carry a figurine of a lion in your pocket to remind you of her presence and support when you must "do battle."

EOS

"Eos rose into the sky from the river Okeanos (Oceanus) at the start of each day, and with her rays of light dispersed the mists of night."

—www.theoi.com

HISTORY AND MYTHOLOGY

Eos, the Greek goddess of dawn, is known in Roman mythology as Aurora. Daughter of Theia and Hyperion, sister to the moon goddess Selene and the sun god Helios, she emerged from the ocean each morning and drove her golden, horse-drawn chariot into the sky to herald the day. Some legends say she followed her brother Helios throughout the day as he lit up the world.

Eos married Astraeus, god of dusk, and together they had several children who some sources describe as the winds, the evening star, and the planets known in ancient times. She also had two sons with the Trojan prince Theonus. One named Memnon was killed by Achilles in the Trojan War, and legend says Eos's tears for her dead son turned into drops of morning dew.

According to myth, Eos slept with Ares, Aphrodite's longtime lover (who was also her brother), and the angry Aphrodite put a curse on Eos. From then on, Eos was plagued with insatiable lust and couldn't resist falling in love with handsome mortals. One of her legendary lovers was a young man named Cephalus, who happened to be happily married. The goddess tricked him into accidentally killing his wife and taking up with her. Eos's most famous love affair, however, was with the hunter and demigod, Orion.

VIRTUES

Eos is usually depicted as a beautiful woman, often wearing a pink or flowered gown to represent the morning. Some images show her with feathered wings that change colors in the growing light. As goddess of the dawn, she symbolizes hope and new beginnings. During the Trojan War, she encouraged the Trojans with her beams of light.

Infamous for her passion and promiscuity, Eos made enemies among both deities and earthly women. However, she also showed loyalty to one of her human mates, Theonus, and asked Zeus to make him immortal (forgetting to ask that he remain forever young). Eos continued to nurse him into extreme old age until she could no longer bear to see him suffer. At her request, Zeus transformed Theonus into a cicada that would chirp each day at the break of dawn.

MANIFESTING HER POWER

When you feel discouraged and don't think you can carry on, or you can't see the way clearly, ask Eos to shine her light into the darkness. Go outside at daybreak and look to the east. As the first pink rays of morning creep above the horizon, sense the goddess bringing you a new dawn. Feel the hope and encouragement she offers. Note in your journal the thoughts and impressions you receive as the sky grows bright and Eos's chariot rises into the heavens.

Lusty Eos can also help enhance your sex life. If the passion has gone out of a romantic relationship, ask the goddess to offer you some tips to stoke the fires again. Of all the Olympian goddesses, Eos probably understood mortal men best. Wear bright rose-colored garments and decorate your home with pink roses to connect with the deity's sensual nature.

ERESHKIGAL

"Ereshkigal is like Kali, who through time and suffering 'pitilessly grinds down…all distinctions…in her indiscriminating fires'—and yet heaves forth new life."

—Sylvia Brinton Perera, *Descent to the Goddess*

HISTORY AND MYTHOLOGY

Sumer's goddess of Attalu, the land of the dead, Ereshkigal is a terrifying deity whose name means "Lady of the Great Place Below." She ruled the underworld, passing judgment on those who'd left the land of the living, and was one of the most feared—and respected—of the Sumerian deities. Reputedly, she lived in a palace made of lapis lazuli that was guarded by seven gates.

According to one myth, she originally reigned supreme in her dark land, but she fell in love with the war god Nergal who visited Attalu to bring an offering of food and drink. Ereshkigal invited him to stay and rule alongside her for six months of the year. He was the only one of her four consorts who agreed to remain in her underworld.

Ancient epic poems describe Ereshkigal's harshness toward her beautiful sister Inanna, a vain and self-serving love goddess who ruled heaven and earth. As the story goes, Inanna descended into the underworld for the funeral of the god Gugulana (whose death she caused), but Ereshkigal wasn't happy to see her sister. She demanded that her sister remove clothing and jewelry at each of the palace's seven gates, until she stood naked and humbled before the Queen of the Dead. For Inanna's crimes, Ereshkigal executed her and hung her body on a hook on a wall.

Inanna's servant, Ninshubur, pleaded with other deities in the Sumerian pantheon to release the goddess from the underworld, which they eventually did, but Inanna's partner, Dumuzi, had to take her place in the land of the dead.

VIRTUES

Some sources connect Ereshkigal with the crone, or the wise older woman. However, she's often depicted as a bitter, angry deity whose vindictiveness drives her to behave cruelly. Early writings describe her as a formidable and frightening goddess linked with fate, justice, and retribution. She brought even the highest and mightiest to their knees, as she did her own sister. No one escaped her ultimate decision. Consequently, she maintained order on earth.

A nearly 4,000-year-old relief sculpture known as the Burney Relief, often interpreted as depicting Ereshkigal, presents an image of a nude woman with wings, accompanied by owls and standing on the backs of two lions that may represent wisdom and power/rulership respectively.

MANIFESTING HER POWER

When you're required to make a difficult decision, ask Ereshkigal to guide you. She's the goddess of "tough love" and will lend her support when you must come down hard on someone you care about, for his or her own good. Wear lapis lazuli jewelry, the stone from which her palace was made, to strengthen your resolve and support healing.

Have you been selfish? Arrogant? Hurtful toward others? Ask Ereshkigal to teach you humility. Prostrate yourself before her and promise to behave better in the future. To gain the goddess's support, commit an act of atonement, such as apologizing or offering payback for an unkindness. Enjoy the freedom that comes from your admission.

ERIS

"Our real discoveries come from chaos, from going to the place that looks wrong and stupid and foolish."
—Chuck Palahniuk, *Invisible Monsters*

HISTORY AND MYTHOLOGY

Considering the notoriously tempestuous marriage between the Greek deities Zeus and Hera, it's no surprise that the couple would spawn the daughter Eris, goddess of strife, chaos, and discord. (Her Roman equivalent goes by the name Discordia.) Wherever this goddess went she stirred up trouble. Some stories even say she hovered over battlefields, enjoying the violence.

She also liked to instigate rivalry. One famous legend associated with her is the Judgment of Paris, which pitted the three most beautiful Greek goddesses—Hera, Aphrodite, and Athena—against one another. She initiated the contest (and its many ramifications) because she didn't get an invitation to the wedding of Peleus and Thetis (parents of Achilles). Out of spite for not being included in the wedding celebration, Eris tossed a golden apple with the word *kaliste*, "to the fairest," inscribed on it into the group of celebrants.

As the sister of Ares, god of war, Eris relished the turmoil and anguish of battle. The Greek poet Hesiod described her children as representatives of humankind's misfortunes—she even named one of her sons Strife. In other sources, she birthed the goddess Gaia (earth), the sky god Ouranos, and Hades (lord of the underworld).

VIRTUES

Contemporary psychologists would describe Eris as having come from a dysfunctional family, and the constant sparring between her Olympian parents led her to become the goddess of marital discord. Historians, poets, and artists usually depict her in unflattering ways, to say the least. Few seem to like this bad-tempered goddess very much.

Some sources, however, paint Eris in a more positive way. By sparking jealousy and competition in mortals, she pushes people to strive harder and encourages them to better themselves. She forces human beings to see what's wrong in their lives, to face their faults, and take responsibility for their bad behavior. She represents what psychoanalyst Carl Jung called "the shadow": the dark, hidden, unlovable part in each of us that we don't want to acknowledge. Viewed in this way, Eris serves as a mirror that reflects what we don't want to see so that we can correct it.

MANIFESTING HER POWER

It may seem that Eris is the last goddess whose power you'd want to call upon, but even this unlikable deity has something to offer. If your life has become too static and you fear making changes, Eris can encourage you to break down the barriers that have kept you trapped. She knows how to handle chaos without losing herself in the process. Choose an object that represents your limitations, then destroy it to symbolize your newfound freedom.

Do you shy away from competition? Do you hide your power because you're afraid to confront an adversary or stir up animosity in some area of your life? Are you letting someone else take advantage of you? If so, ask Eris to give you the strength to "do battle" with the opposition. Stand before your mirror and ask the goddess to reveal your dark side to you, to help you see the unresolved anger, jealousy, and mean-spiritedness that lie within. Don't judge yourself, just observe your feelings. The simple act of acknowledging them is a first step. Until we face the unappealing facets of our personalities, we can't put them to rest.

FREYA

"The ninth Battle-Plain, where bright Freya / Decides
where the warriors shall sit: / Half of the fallen follow
the goddess, / And half belong to Odin."
—*The Elder Edda: A Selection*, "The Lay of Grimnir,"
translated by W.H. Auden and P.B. Taylor

HISTORY AND MYTHOLOGY

Mythology tells us the Norse/Germanic goddess Freya brought light and fire to the people of Northern Europe. Her name means "lady" and is spelled in various ways, including Freija, Frøjya, and Frejya. A fiery deity, she's linked with the flames of the hearth and forge as well as with sexual passion. Freya reputedly taught her female prophetesses and followers the dance of ecstasy, which enabled them to divine the future.

The exquisitely beautiful daughter of Njord, god of the wind, waves, sailors, and the coastal regions, and his sister Nerthus, Freya had a twin brother named Freyr. Legends say she married the god Ord, but it's possible she actually wed Odin (some sources say they're two names for the same deity), and had two children, Hnoss and Gersimi. She hails from the world of Vanir, one of the nine realms suspended in the great tree Yggdrasil.

Freya, however, isn't only a love goddess. She also plays a key role in warfare. During a war waged by the two tribes Vanir and the Aesir, Freya was sent to the Aesir (the better-known clan to which Odin belonged) to cement a truce between the two nations. Folklore says that whenever soldiers die in battle, she chooses half of the fallen men and ushers them into the afterlife; the others are consigned to Odin's great hall in Valhalla.

VIRTUES

Artists often show Freya riding across the heavens in her chariot drawn by two cats. She can also fly on her own if she wishes, due to a magic cape she wears made from the feathers of falcons. Usually she's depicted with golden hair from which flowers fall, and her tears are the colors gold and amber.

Legend tells us the sensuous Freya loves jewelry, fine clothing, and other beautiful things, and that she often used her beauty to acquire the luxuries she adored. Most precious of her treasures was the magnificent golden necklace of the Brisingamen, which she acquired by trading sexual pleasures to four dwarves.

Adept in the Norse magic known as *seidr*, Freya knows how to weave the web of destiny to direct the course of life on earth. As such, she has connections to the Norns, the three wise women who spin the thread of life, measure it, and cut it.

MANIFESTING HER POWER

Freya teaches the art of sexual love. She can show you how to express your sensuality more joyfully and give pleasure to a partner. Call on her to help you appreciate the creative power of sexual union and to honor the divine nature of that which brings forth life. Rub amber resin on your pulse points to enhance your attractiveness and sensuality.

A "material girl," Freya can help you acquire wealth. Study the practice of sex magic, which taps sexual energy to produce material outcomes, in order to attract greater abundance in your life. In Norse tradition, deities ruled over the days of the week. Friday is Freya's day, so petition her for assistance on Fridays. In return for her aid, offer her a gift of amber jewelry.

FRIGG

"Chains do not hold a marriage together. It is
threads, hundreds of tiny threads,
which sew people together through the years."
—Simone Signoret, French actress

HISTORY AND MYTHOLOGY

Wife to the powerful father-god Odin, Frigg (or Frigga) was the Norse goddess of love, marriage, and fertility. Her name means "beloved." Legend tells us she gave birth to Baldur, god of light, on the Winter Solstice, the longest night of the year in the northern hemisphere.

Mythology also describes her as a seer and connects her with fate. Like the Greek Moirai, she wove the destinies of humankind, and of the deities as well. When she foresaw the death of her son, the loving mother goddess pleaded with all things on earth not to harm Baldur. However, she overlooked the simple mistletoe plant. The trickster god, Loki, took advantage of this and dipped an arrow in the poisonous plant's juice, then gave it to Baldur's blind brother Hodor, god of darkness. While pretending to teach Hodor to use the weapon, Loki guided the poisoned arrow toward Baldur, killing him.

In some versions of the story, Baldur came back to life. The grateful Frigg changed mistletoe's associations from a deadly plant to the one we connect with love and kiss under today.

VIRTUES

Foremost among the Norse goddesses, the beautiful Frigg birthed both light and darkness. Her myth represents the changing seasons, the waxing and waning of the sun's power through the year, giving her dominion over them. It also describes the ongoing cycle of birth, death, and rebirth.

Her delivery of Baldur at the Winter Solstice, thereby bringing light and hope into the world at the darkest and bleakest time, has parallels to the story of Jesus's birth and Christmas.

As a devoted mother, Frigg protects women in labor and their infants during birth. As the wife of the highest-ranking god in the Norse pantheon, she also governs love and marriage.

Her role as goddess of destiny shows her weaving the web of fate. She could change the course of human destiny by reweaving portions of the web. And as a weaver, she's also in charge of the domestic arts.

Germanic folklore tells us the goose was sacred to Frigg, and therefore these tales connect her with the storybook character Mother Goose. Reputedly she caused snow to fall when she shook out her goose-down comforter. Legends show a close connection between Frigg and Freya—and in some cases mix (and muddle) the two goddesses' characteristics, powers, and behavior.

MANIFESTING HER POWER

This mother goddess can aid those who wish to become pregnant. On the eve of the Winter Solstice, light a white candle in her honor and let it burn down completely to solicit her assistance. Frigg can help you attract a loving partner or guide a romance to fulfillment in marriage. Seek her assistance, too, if a relationship has hit a rough spot and you want to restore peace and harmony. Hang a sprig of mistletoe above the entrance to your home to enhance affectionate feelings. Send prayers to Frigg the first night after the new moon to encourage positive growth and new beginnings in your love life.

GAIA

"Earth the beautiful rose up / Broad-bosomed, she that is the
steadfast base / Of all things. And fair Earth first bore /
The starry Heaven, equal to herself, / To cover her on all sides
and to be / A home forever for the blessed gods."

—Hesiod, Greek poet

HISTORY AND MYTHOLOGY

The oldest and most important of the Greek goddesses, Gaia (or Gaea, Terra in Roman myth) predates the Greco-Roman period and harkens back to ancient matriarchal cultures. She's the primal Mother Goddess, Mother Nature, Mother Earth, who both created and presides over everything on our planet. Mythology tells us that at the very beginning, Gaia shaped the earth out of the void and chaos, and fashioned all that exists here in the physical world—an idea similar to the Genesis story of creation. She brought about the sky, Ouranos, and the sea, Pontus. Through her union with Ouranos, she also birthed some of the most notable figures in Greek mythology, including Cronus, Themis, Prometheus, and the Titans.

Gaia's fertility didn't end there, however. She also mothered monsters, including the one-eyed Cyclops and the many-headed Hecatoncheires, as well as the vengeful Erinyes (a.k.a., Furies, who punished wrongdoers), tree nymphs, giants, and thunder and lightning. It was said that virtually everything in heaven and earth owes its origin to this primordial goddess.

VIRTUES

As the ultimate creator goddess, Gaia is responsible for having brought humanity into being. We are all her children. She reigns over earth and sky, bridges body and mind, and governs the natural world and the realm of the spirits. In short, she's the source of all we know.

In early earth-honoring cultures, people offered honey cakes and other food gifts to Gaia to thank her or petition her aid in bringing about a bountiful harvest. Artists often depict Gaia as a voluptuous, matronly woman (suggesting her fertility), sometimes garbed in green or with fruit and vegetables (to show her guardianship of nature). We see her image in the Venus of Willendorf, the oldest known sculpture of a human form, estimated to date back more than 25,000 years.

MANIFESTING HER POWER

Because of her unlimited fertility, women who wish to become pregnant can ask Gaia for assistance. To gain her favor, leave food offerings outdoors in a place you consider sacred, as our ancestors did (the birds and animals will appreciate your generosity).

If your goal is to attract abundance (financial or otherwise), let Gaia help you manifest your intention. Consider planting "seed money" by donating to an environmental cause in Gaia's name. Visualize the money coming back to you threefold.

Do something to benefit nature, and you'll tap into Gaia's fruitful energy. Plant flowers, a garden, or perhaps a tree. Instead of using chemicals on your yard, go organic. Spend more time outdoors and live in constant appreciation of earth's beauty. Notice how connecting with the natural world helps you feel calmer and more content.

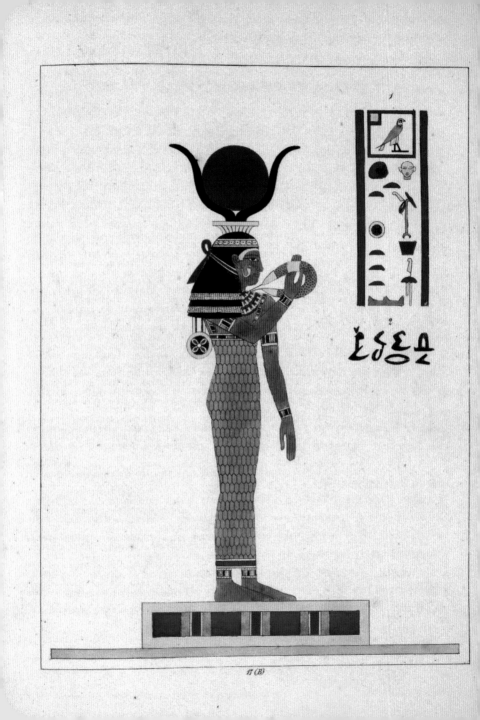

HATHOR

"Hathor was the golden goddess who helped women to give birth, the dead to be reborn, and the cosmos to be renewed."
—Geraldine Pinch, *Egyptian Mythology: A Guide to the Gods, Goddesses, and Traditions of Ancient Egypt*

HISTORY AND MYTHOLOGY

As one of ancient Egypt's most important goddesses, Hathor governed love, beauty, music, and happiness—in short, all the good things in life. It's said she liked to dance, but she wasn't just a party girl. She also came to the aid of women during childbirth and protected the dead on their journey into the afterlife. Her appreciation of life, her joyful nature, and her role as a female who celebrates love as wife, mother, and companion made her a revered goddess among women. She is often associated with the Greeks' Aphrodite and the Romans' Venus.

In her role as a patroness of women, she also assumed the path of nurturer, midwife, guardian, and healer. Mythology says that "Seven Hathors" were present at each child's birth, and these deities consigned the newborn soul to its fate. With red ribbons, they bound up evil spirits who might seek to harm the infant or its mother.

Despite Hathor's focus on motherhood and matrimony, she's not to be considered subservient to any male deity. One legend says she left the home of her father, the sun god Ra, to experience a wilder, freer existence. When he attempted to rein her in, Hathor caused the Nile to overflow, and ever since, the river's life-giving waters signify her powerful, creative properties.

Over time, some of the stories about Hathor have gotten muddied and mixed in with those of other Egyptian goddesses, including Isis.

VIRTUES

Hathor is usually linked with cows, which represent her maternal and protective qualities. Depictions of the goddess often show her wearing a headdress with curved horns that hold the disc of the sun between them. In her role as goddess of beauty, she favored the use of cosmetics and aromatics, especially myrrh. One of her favorite symbols was a hand mirror, which resembles the ankh and the glyph for Venus. According to mythology, Hathor's image could be found as a decoration on women's mirrors.

Mythology also connects the goddess with precious metals and gems, especially turquoise and malachite. Early Egyptians adorned their eyes with crushed malachite, prized not only for its aesthetic properties, but also for its ability to protect against eye infections. Therefore, Hathor served as patroness of the gem mines in the Sinai Peninsula.

The goddess, as well as her priests and priestesses, wore a beaded collar-like necklace known as a menat, which may have held magical significance. Early Egyptian mortals had a fondness for these necklaces too, and those who could afford them wore them proudly. Some sources suggest the menat could also have been a percussion instrument, used in connection with a sistrum (a type of rattle).

MANIFESTING HER POWER

If you or someone you know will soon have a baby, invite Hathor to attend the birth. In the birthing room, place an image of the goddess or a figurine of a cow to represent her. If you wish, drink milk or eat another dairy product in her honor. She'll offer protection and blessings to mother and child.

Hathor can also assist you in matters of the heart. Ask her to help you attract a romantic partner or to increase the joy in an existing relationship. If you are feeling stuck or in a rut, play music and dance to honor the goddess. Let her spirit help you feel more beautiful and alive. Paint your eyes in turquoise or malachite-green eye shadow, dab on a little myrrh essential oil, or don a menat necklace as a good luck charm.

HECATE

"The Greek goddess Hecate reminds us of the importance of change, helping us to release the past, especially those things that are hindering our growth, and to accept change and transitions."
—Sharon Turnbull, www.goddessgift.com

HISTORY AND MYTHOLOGY

One of the most mysterious and formidable of the Greek goddesses, Hecate can be found at the "crossroads," the place where decisions must be made and paths chosen. She's called the Goddess of the Dark Moon, and the ancient Romans knew her as Trivia. There's nothing trivial about this deity, however. She's been there, done that, grown wise through countless experiences, and no longer fears the darkness of the underworld. In the myth of Persephone, Hecate came to Demeter's aid when Hades kidnapped her daughter, and Hecate accompanied Persephone on her annual journey into the underworld.

As the only child of the Titan war god Perses and the star goddess Asteria, Hecate was worshipped by the people of Athens. In fact, they erected shrines to her in return for her gifts of protection and prosperity. Legend says she had the power to grant humans anything they wished, or to withhold it from them if she chose. The Greek poet Hesiod tells us Zeus held Hecate in high regard and allotted her parts of the earth, the sea, and the starry sky.

Hecate is familiar with spirits, ghosts, and the world of the dead. In her role as a protector deity, she's often depicted with two ghostly dogs that bark a warning when an attack is imminent. As Queen of the Night, Hecate moves comfortably through the spirit realm and the land of dreams, and she's sometimes shown with an owl as a companion. One legend says she lived on the edge of reality, where she was accompanied

by ghosts as well as social outcasts, including slaves who'd been released from bondage to serve her.

VIRTUES

Hecate depicts the crone aspect of the Triple Goddess, the wise elder. Unlike Athena, who's known for her intellectual acumen and ingenuity, Hecate possesses occult knowledge, intuition, and the gift of prophecy. The patroness of witches, Hecate teaches the secrets of magic and healing. Herbalism is her specialty, and legend says she was an expert at crafting botanical medicines as well as poisons. Not surprisingly, she is linked to the yew tree, as the tree lives a long time and is seen as a symbol of death and rebirth.

A solitary deity, she treasures her independence and doesn't need a husband to take care of her—she's a protector goddess, after all. She trusts her own wisdom and honors her own truth.

MANIFESTING HER POWER

In the midst of a transition, seek the wise counsel of Hecate. When you must go to a place that scares you, ask Hecate to accompany you. Place three stones at an intersection to mark the crossroads, the site of your brave decision and your adventure into the unknown.

Because Hecate understands the spirit world and the ongoing cycle of life, death, and rebirth, she can give you strength when you must face the passing of someone dear to you—or your own transition. She assures you that physical death is not the end, only another step in the ongoing journey of the soul's evolution. Make an amulet of basil, comfrey, and rosemary to bless the person's passage, and trust that all is well.

If you've chosen to tread a magical path, invite Hecate to serve as your teacher. Light a black candle in her honor. Record your dreams in a journal or book of shadows—they may contain messages from the goddess.

HEL

"[Hel] has the power to dole out lodgings and provisions to those who are sent to her, and they are the people who have died of disease or old age....Her hall is called Eljudnir...her dish is Hunger, her knife is Famine, her slave is Lazy, and Slothful is her woman servant....Mostly she is gloomy and cruel."

—Snorri Sturluson, *The Prose Edda*, "Gylfaginning 34"

HISTORY AND MYTHOLOGY

Mythology depicts the Norse goddess Hel as a giantess who ruled the underworld, known as the Halls of Hel. Her name means "hidden," and the saying "go to Hel" meant to die. The daughter of the trickster god Loki and the giantess Angrboda (whose name translates to "one who brings grief"), she's also the sister of Fenrir, the wolf, and Jormungandr, the serpent—your ultimate dysfunctional family.

Not everyone who died ended up in Hel's vast underground realm, one of the nine worlds in Norse mythology. As the thirteenth-century *Prose Edda* tells us, only those who succumbed to illness or old age went there. (Some sources suggest disease first entered the world when Hel was born.) Warriors who died valiantly in battle were whisked off to Valhalla by the goddess Freya and the Valkyries instead.

According to one story, Hel's father killed Baldur, the beloved god of light and the son of Frigg and Odin, with a poisoned arrow. Everyone grieved his passing, so the gods sent a messenger into the underworld to negotiate Baldur's return. The arrogant goddess wanted to keep her prize and refused, unless everything in the world—living and dead—wept for the imprisoned god. Although virtually all shed tears, one giantess named Thokk (who may have been Loki in disguise) stubbornly held out, insisting she'd never liked Baldur anyway.

VIRTUES

Usually Hel gets a bad rap in legends, as she is said to be harsh, grim, gloomy, greedy, bad-tempered, and cruel. According to myth, she reigned over an underground realm where she had many mansions with high walls and countless servants to do her bidding.

Some sources show her as half black and half white. Others describe her as a mix of blue and the pale color of Norse skin. Others say her skeleton protruded out of one side of her body. Her piebald coloring brings to mind the Chinese yin-yang symbol that represents a whole formed of dark and light. Thus, Hel signifies the conscious and unconscious, the "known" side of an individual and the "shadow."

Jacob Grimm (of fairytale fame) likened Hel to Kali, the Hindu goddess of death, and described her as a "black goddess." Grimm also called her "a harbinger of plague and pestilence" who rode a three-legged horse across the land, snatching up the souls she determined belonged to her.

MANIFESTING HER POWER

Although you may wonder why anyone would want to make a connection with such an unpleasant goddess, Hel—like all deities and all humans—has an important role to play. She can show you how to face your shadow side—the part of yourself that you don't like or want to acknowledge—and integrate it into your personality. Find a white stone and paint half of it black. Hold it during meditation to solicit Hel's aid in confronting your flaws.

People who grew up in dysfunctional families or who have suffered ridicule because they were "different" can turn to Hel to help them understand feelings of anger, vindictiveness, depression, and isolation. Light two candles, one white and one black, to honor her. Ask her to let you realize that you have gifts to offer and that people do care about you. Let Hel help you accept that despite your perceived failings, you are worthy of respect and joy.

HERA

"Have no fear if you are righteous...tremble if you're not....Hera is nearer than you think."

—www.mythagora.com

HISTORY AND MYTHOLOGY

Called Queen of Heaven, Hera was the daughter of the Greek deities Cronus and Rhea. Her counterpart in Roman mythology is Juno. Some sources say she predates ancient Greece and was derived from earlier matriarchal societies. As the wife and sister of Zeus, Hera is known as the goddess of marriage, although her own marriage to the famously unfaithful Zeus was often rocky. Mythology tells us she only married him because he'd tricked her by pretending to be a cuckoo and then raped her, and she wanted to cover up her embarrassment.

Zeus made a lot of enemies among the Olympians, and when Hera decided to rebel against her husband, she enlisted their help in binding him. However, Briareus, whom Zeus had saved from a dragon, freed the god. As punishment, Zeus chained his wife in the heavens where she cried all night until he finally relented and let her down, on the condition that she never again try to overthrow him.

The licentious Zeus engaged in numerous infidelities, which enflamed Hera's notorious jealousy. When she discovered his lover Leto was pregnant with Artemis and Apollo, Hera chased Leto away to an island. She took vengeance on Zeus's illegitimate son Hercules too, and tormented him in numerous ways. Hera had several children with Zeus, including the war god Ares and Eris, goddess of discord.

According to Homer's *Iliad*, Hera played a key role in the Trojan War, working tirelessly on the side of Greece to defeat the Trojans. The goddess even descended from Mount Olympus to fight on the battlefield.

VIRTUES

A goddess of great beauty, Hera competed against Aphrodite and Athena in the divine beauty contest known as the Judgment of Paris—and she should've won, had Aphrodite not bribed Paris. Hera never forgave this injustice. It only fueled her anger toward Paris's home city of Troy.

Although many legends focus on Hera's jealousy and her vindictiveness toward Zeus's lovers and their offspring, she remained faithful to her husband. Therefore, she signifies fidelity in marriage. Her fierceness arose from righteous indignation, which she directed at those she felt had wronged her. Known for her loyalty, she protected and aided those who befriended or helped her.

Hera is often associated with peacocks, symbols of pride and beauty. She is sometimes depicted riding in a chariot drawn by the magnificent birds. Legend also connects her with the cow, an animal frequently linked with motherhood and nourishment. Sometimes she's shown holding a pomegranate that represents fertility.

MANIFESTING HER POWER

If you're in a difficult marriage or relationship, Hera can give you the strength to continue in the partnership and overcome the challenges. Make an offering to her of pomegranates (or pomegranate juice). She can also show you how to stand up for yourself if you feel you're being taken advantage of—however, you probably don't want to follow her example of retaliating with hurtful behavior. Draw from her strength instead of her anger.

Hera can also help you appreciate your own beauty. Regardless of popular images of beauty, each of us has attractive qualities, inside and out. Ask Hera to show you how to express yours with aplomb. Acquire a peacock feather to remind you of the goddess and hold it when you need self-confidence.

HESTIA

"Each city too had a public hearth sacred to Hestia, where the fire was never allowed to go out."

—Edith Hamilton, *Mythology*

HISTORY AND MYTHOLOGY

Known as the Greek goddess of the hearth and temple, Hestia's Roman counterpart is Vesta. She was the firstborn of the deities Rhea and Cronus, sister to Zeus, Hera, Demeter, Poseidon, and Hades. Considered one of the "virgin" goddesses, she chose not to have a husband and independently pursued what mattered most to her. She shunned male attention and withdrew to a quiet life of contemplation. Mythology tells us both the sea god Poseidon and the handsome sun deity Apollo loved her, but Hestia rejected their affections.

She also turned her back on power, prestige, and possessions. As a result, she managed to stay out of the convoluted conflicts, romantic affairs, and ego dynamics that engulfed many of the other Olympians. Instead, she concerned herself with domestic life. Despite her lack of glamor, many Greeks honored Hestia with prayers before meals and with rituals at significant life events such as childbirth.

Legends conflict about whether to include her as one of the Twelve Olympians, perhaps because, as some sources suggest, she gave up her position to the more assertive Dionysius in order to ease tension among the deities.

VIRTUES

Hestia eschews the drama of goddesses such as Hera, and although she demonstrates kindness and nurturing qualities, she remains emotionally reserved. She's comfortable with her own company and enjoys solitude. On one hand, she's the temple priestess, the nun, keeper of sacred rituals and spiritual life. On the other hand, she focuses on ordinary, everyday tasks in the home with an attitude of mindfulness, making them her meditation, and thus injects peace and harmony into all she does.

As goddess of the hearth, Hestia is linked with fire. Because early hearths were usually round, her symbol is the circle, which also represents wholeness. In ancient Greece, the hearth was both the place for food preparation and for making offerings to the deities. Homer wrote of Hestia, "among all mortals she was chief of the goddesses."

We also associate Hestia with the wise woman archetype. From her elevated, detached position she's capable of acting without ego, in a calm, steady, peaceful way that brings order to everyday existence. In human life she's represented as the elder, dominant woman in the household who holds everything together.

MANIFESTING HER POWER

When you need to detach from the stress of everyday life, ask Hestia to guide you. Practicing mindfulness, or conscious awareness of being in the present moment, is a good way to channel Hestia's spirit. To do this, focus your attention on each action you undertake—especially ordinary tasks such as washing dishes or folding laundry—and see it as a sacred function of being in the world.

At mealtime, offer thanks to Hestia for the simple comforts and blessings in your life. Spend time each day in meditation to quiet your mind and quell the ego's demand for dominance. Notice when your emotions are interfering with your common sense—take a few deep breaths and ask Hestia to help you step back and view things from a wise woman's perspective.

INANNA

"Inanna (later Ishtar of the Assyrians) was among the most popular deities and may have inspired similar goddesses in many other cultures."

—www.ancient.eu

HISTORY AND MYTHOLOGY

Mythology connects the ancient Sumerian mother goddess Inanna, called the Queen of Heaven, with love, sex, fertility, and beauty. She's one of the world's oldest goddesses and early epics gave her dominion over the underworld as well as heaven and earth (later myths put her sister Ereshkigal in charge of the Land of the Dead). Contemporary sources suggest Ereshkigal may represent the dark or "shadow" side of Inanna.

In her role as a fertility goddess, Inanna and her consort Dumuzi entered into "sacred marriage" each fall (the rainy season in Sumer) to encourage the earth's abundance. Legend says Dumuzi died each summer, when the harsh sun burned up the crops, and he descended into the underworld.

In one well-known story, Inanna entered the underworld where her sister reigned. There, Inanna was stripped of her status and subjected to humiliation, forced at each of the seven gates of Ereshkigal's palace to give up more of her clothing, possessions, and self-esteem until she was brought naked and vulnerable before the Queen of the Dead. Some sources say Ereshkigal was jealous of her beautiful sister, while others believe Inanna was responsible for the death of Sumer's bull god and had to pay for her crime. Whatever the reason, Ereshkigal killed her sister and hung her on a hook on a wall. Eventually, however, Ereshkigal allowed Inanna to return to her own realm (otherwise everything on earth would've ceased to exist) with the condition that someone else take her place. Dumuzi was chosen.

VIRTUES

Sometimes depicted with wings, Inanna was beautiful beyond words. The Queen of Heaven wore a rainbow necklace and a girdle of stars. She's also associated with the planet Venus and the moon. As goddess of the earth, she oversaw crops, trees, and livestock. As a fertility deity, she's linked with sexuality and sensuality. Some myths describe her as indulgent, vain, and self-centered, mainly concerned with enjoying pleasure and luxuries.

The story of her descent into the underworld, however, reveals another side to Inanna: her courage and perseverance as she worked her way through Ereshkigal's seven gates, divesting herself of her possessions and her pride.

MANIFESTING HER POWER

Ask this beautiful fertility goddess to increase your creative powers and to improve your artistic ability. She can also teach you the secrets of sacred sexuality and how to deepen your relationship with an intimate partner. Place a vase of roses, Inanna's favorite flowers, in your bedroom as a gift to her.

The myth of Inanna suggests the cycle of the seasons as well as the cycle of life, death, and rebirth. In psychological terms, it can symbolize going into yourself to meet your inner darkness.

Inanna can guide you in your quest to understand yourself better—especially your "shadow" side. If you must let go of things you feel attached to, the goddess can help you release old habits, behaviors, material objects, or people that may be hindering your personal growth. Remove your clothing and jewelry, stand naked before your mirror, and ask the goddess to lend you her strength, grace, and humility to surrender to the greater good.

IRIS

"Life throws challenges and every challenge comes with rainbows and lights to conquer it."

—Amit Ray, *World Peace: The Voice of a Mountain Bird*

HISTORY AND MYTHOLOGY

The daughter of the sea god Thaumas and the cloud/sky nymph Elektra, the Greek deity Iris is known as the Goddess of the Rainbow. Her heritage describes our earth's cycle of precipitation and evaporation, and the relationship between the ocean, the land, and the sky. Early legends describe her as a virgin goddess; however, later stories say she married Zephyrus, god of the west wind, and birthed Eros, the god of desire.

Mythology also portrays her as a divine messenger and the handmaiden of the goddess Hera, Queen of Heaven. Iris's role not only involves conveying messages back and forth between the Olympian deities but also from the gods and goddesses to human beings. The message she brings is one of peace and hope, signified by the beautiful rainbow. Mythology often showcases Hermes (Mercury in Roman texts) as the messenger god, but Iris's symbolism suggests she's something more. She's not just a divine letter carrier; she also serves as a benevolent mediator and a cosmic cheerleader who brings good tidings.

VIRTUES

Iris blends the symbols of emotion (water) and intellect (air). Some images show her with wings (signifying her connection with the clouds/sky through her mother) and carrying a pitcher of water (to represent her father's watery nature). Therefore, she's ideally suited to handle emotional communications between lovers, to resolve romantic disputes, to give shape to intuition, and to direct creative pursuits.

Sometimes shown standing between Zeus and Hera and offering the feuding couple nectar, Iris suggests sharing the sweetness between you and your partner, releasing the hurts. She's also depicted in art and literature holding a caduceus, symbol of healing, which likely signifies healing the emotions as the precursor to healing the body. The rainbow represents peace and joy after a storm, therefore Iris promises hope and happy endings.

MANIFESTING HER POWER

After a rainstorm, go outside and find a rainbow in the sky. Make a wish and ask Iris to assist you in bringing your fondest dream to fruition. Watch the rainbow until it gradually disappears, and then give thanks for the blessings you're about to receive.

If you feel alienated from someone you love or have something you want to say to a loved one, ask Iris to help you bridge the gap. Write a letter to the person with whom you wish to connect, expressing your feelings honestly and stating your desire for a positive resolution to your problem. Draw a rainbow on the letter to symbolize your hopes and dreams for a bright future. You may not even need to mail the letter—sometimes just putting your heartfelt thoughts out into the universe is enough. Let Iris carry your intentions to the person with whom you wish to communicate.

Draw a rainbow on a piece of paper. Notice that each of its seven colors corresponds to one of the body's seven major energy chakras, according to Eastern healing philosophy. If you're not already familiar with these, look up their meanings online. Then write on each band of color something you want to express within yourself that corresponds to that chakra's significance.

ISHTAR

"In Babylon, Ishtar encompasses the fullness of womanhood, including being a maternal nurturer, an independent companion, an inspired bed partner, and an insightful advisor in matters of the heart."

—Patricia Telesco, *365 Goddess: A Daily Guide to the Magic and Inspiration of the Goddess*

HISTORY AND MYTHOLOGY

This Mesopotamian goddess shares many characteristics with the earlier Sumerian deity, Inanna, and their stories tend to get mixed in legends over time. Daughter of the sky god Anu (although sometimes said to descend from the moon god Sin), Ishtar was a fertility goddess who governed love and sexuality. Some sources say her temple priestesses engaged in sex with those who sought the goddess's favor. She also exuded power and was considered a deity of war and political power.

Like Inanna, Ishtar descends into the underworld, ruled by Ereshkigal. At each of the seven gates there, Ishtar must take off one piece of clothing until she's presented, naked, to the Queen of the Underworld. Ereshkigal then orders Ishtar imprisoned and plagues her with diseases. Without their fertility goddess, everyone on earth grieves and stops having sex. Ea, god of wisdom, sends a messenger named Asu-shu-namir to the underworld, bearing a container filled with the water of life, and orders Ereshkigal to sprinkle Ishtar with it. Grudgingly she does, healing Ishtar, and the fertility goddess is allowed to go free.

Another story found in the ancient *Epic of Gilgamesh* (and in some legends about Inanna) says Ishtar propositioned the hero Gilgamesh, but he rejected her. In anger, she sent the Bull of Heaven to kill him, but instead Gilgamesh killed the divine bull.

The Gate of Ishtar, built between 605 and 562 B.C.E., stood at the entrance to the city of Babylon and it still exists.

VIRTUES

Among Ishtar's fertility symbols are eggs and rabbits—which Neo-Pagans connect with the goddess Ostare (Eostre) and which Christians link to Easter. Ishtar is pronounced "Easter," although it's unlikely the word Easter derived from her name. Before the fourth century C.E., springtime celebrations in many parts of the world centered around fertility and rebirth.

Associated with the planet Venus, Ishtar often appears with an eight-pointed star to signify her role as the goddess of heaven, but also to symbolize her power (in numerology eight relates to strength). In some depictions, she holds weapons to show she doesn't just make love, she also governs war. Another of her symbols, the lion, represents power too—she's sometimes shown going into battle riding on the back of a lion.

MANIFESTING HER POWER

The dynamic and lusty Ishtar can inspire passion and love. If you'd like to turn up the heat in your love life, invite her to lend you her energy. Ask Ishtar to teach you the art of sacred sex to enhance your relationship. Go outside as night descends and gaze up at the heavens until you spot Venus in the darkening sky—can you sense Ishtar nearby?

Call upon this fertility goddess for aid if you wish to become pregnant. To connect with her power, hard-boil some eggs—symbol of fertility—and share them with your partner.

As a war deity, Ishtar can lend you her courage when you face a challenge or conflict. Acquire a figurine or picture of a lion and carry it with you for courage as you "battle" your adversary.

ISIS

"I, Isis, am all that has been, that is or shall be;
no mortal man hath ever me unveiled."
—Devi Press, www.goddess.ws

HISTORY AND MYTHOLOGY

The Egyptian fertility goddess of marriage, motherhood, and magic, Isis is the daughter of the sky goddess Nut and the earth god Geb. She's also the wife and sister of Osiris and the mother of Horus. One of the most important members of the Egyptian pantheon, her devoted followers included the ancient Greeks and Romans, as well as modern-day pagans.

Perhaps the best-known myth connected with Isis tells us that Set, her brother and god of evil, murdered Osiris and dumped his coffin in the Nile. Heartbroken, Isis searched for her husband and discovered the coffin in another country. When she brought him home, however, Set dismembered the body, ripping it into fourteen pieces that he scattered across the land so Osiris couldn't have a proper burial. Her sister, Nephthys, helped her find all but one piece (his penis), which Isis refashioned from wax. Due to his wife's magical abilities, Osiris came to life again for one night, during which he impregnated Isis with their son Horus.

Another legend says Isis tricked the sun god, Ra, into revealing his secret name. Once the goddess knew this name, she could control him. Ra, at the time, was an old, sick, drooling deity and Isis used his spittle to create a snake (or possibly a scorpion) that bit Ra. She promised to heal him—which she did—but only after he relinquished his throne to her son Horus.

VIRTUES

Because of her devotion to Osiris, Isis is considered the ideal wife. Her ability to bring her husband back to life and conceive a child with him

indicates her magical skill and regenerative power—she holds the key to immortality. Mythology tells us the tears Isis cried over the death of her husband were so copious that they caused the Nile to overflow each year. This annual flooding, which enables crops to grow, is another symbol of her role as a fertility goddess.

Images frequently show Isis with magnificent wings outstretched to guard against evil. Her wings also provided protection for the souls of the deceased. Some sources say she used her wings to fan air back into the body of her murdered husband, thus emphasizing her magical abilities and the power of life over death. She also holds an ankh, symbol of life.

Her name means "throne," and she's often depicted wearing a throne-like headdress. This suggests her connection with the pharaoh, viewed as the divine representative on earth. She's sometimes shown nursing the pharaoh, sometimes Horus—an image that researchers link to Christianity's mother and child.

MANIFESTING HER POWER

As the goddess of marriage, Isis can help you handle relationship problems, especially those related to devotion, fidelity, and renewal. Dedicate a special time each week to do something with your partner that you both enjoy. Celebrate your relationship in small ways often. Make a list of the good things in your relationship and share it with your partner. In addition, Isis teaches that women need not be subservient to their mates; rather, they possess the magic to nurture what's important, create what's essential, and repair what's been damaged on their own.

As a mother goddess, Isis encourages you to nourish, protect, and inspire the child within. What gifts have you neglected? What are you grieving? What's preventing your happiness or success? In meditation, imagine magnificent wings sprouting from your shoulder blades. Ask Isis to help you spread your wings and fly high.

IX CHEL

"The moon is a loyal companion. It never leaves. It's always there, watching, steadfast, knowing us in our light and dark moments, changing forever just as we do."
—Tahereh Mafi, *Shatter Me*

HISTORY AND MYTHOLOGY

Mythology tells us the Mayan fertility goddess Ix Chel nourished the crops by pouring water on the earth from a jar shaped like a womb. Her name means "lady of the rainbow." She was also known as the Mayan moon goddess who fell in love with the sun god Kinich Ahau even though he didn't share the same feelings. Because of her obsession for Kinich Ahau, Ix Chel neglected her duties to earth, which caused devastating weather patterns. Eventually, the talented goddess wove an exquisite cloth that won him over. Together they had four children who became the four directions: North, South, East, West.

Ix Chel didn't have much luck with male deities, though. According to one legend, her grandfather, angry over her marriage, killed her with a lightning bolt. However, she rose from the dead after six months (symbolizing the fertile and barren seasons of the year) and returned to her husband. Kinich Ahau, who was known for his bad temper, threw the goddess out of heaven because he mistakenly thought she was cheating on him. In time, he brought her back, but soon reverted to his old behavior.

Realizing she could never change him, Ix Chel left to live on Isla Mujeres (meaning "Island of Women"), a tiny island in the Caribbean off the coast of the Yucatán Peninsula. There she cared for women during pregnancy and childbirth. Whenever her sun god husband came looking for her, she shape-shifted into a jaguar and hid from him.

VIRTUES

Depictions of Ix Chel often show her upending a jug and pouring water from it. The image represents her dual responsibilities: nourishing the earth with life-giving rain and assisting women in childbirth. Sometimes she wears a snake (symbol of medicine) curled on her head to signify her skill as a healer. She's also portrayed as a weaver, not only of cloth but of life as well. By entwining cosmic threads, she produces the fabric of destiny.

As goddess of the moon, she governs women's fertility cycles. The moon's phases influence the ocean's tides too, and according to legend, flooding occurred when Ix Chel chased the sun god across the sky.

MANIFESTING HER POWER

Healers—especially midwives and obstetricians—can look to Ix Chel as their patron. Ask her to share her knowledge with you and to assist you as you offer healing to others. Women, in particular, who need healing can call upon the goddess for aid. Let her wise counsel comfort you during a pregnancy and birth, or with fertility issues. To connect with Ix Chel's power, write a request for healing on the day of the full moon, then fill a womb-shaped vessel with water and pour the water onto a plant as you speak your request aloud.

Ix Chel can offer courage and solace to abused women or those who find themselves in unhappy relationships. If you're thinking about leaving an unhealthy situation, ask the goddess for guidance by praying or meditating. Allow your mind to quiet and listen to her wise counsel. She can teach you how to conceal yourself from unwanted attention. Acquire an image of a rainbow, perhaps a small stained-glass piece to hang in a window, to encourage hope and connect you with Ix Chel's strength.

IZANAMI-NO-MIKOTO

"For life and death are one, even as the river and the sea are one."
—Kahlil Gibran, *The Prophet*

HISTORY AND MYTHOLOGY

Mythology describes this Japanese goddess as having dominion over life and death. According to legend, she and her husband Izanagi-no-Mikoto created the first landmass on earth, in the region we now know as Japan. To do so, they stood on the bridge that connects heaven and earth and stirred the sea (symbol of the feminine force) beneath them with a magic spear (symbol of the masculine force).

They then took up residence on the island they'd created, called Ono-goro. Soon after, Izanami-no-Mikoto gave birth to the other islands in the Japanese archipelago. She also created the gods and goddesses who would rule the land, seas, plants, winds, rivers, and everything else on earth. When Izanami gave birth to the fire god, however, the baby burned her so badly that she died. Her death introduced physical death into the human world.

The goddess's bereaved husband, Izanagi, killed the fiery child who'd caused his wife's painful demise and followed Izanami into the realm of the dead. There he found the goddess's corpse decomposing and realized she was beyond rescuing. She remained in the underworld and ruled there. Upon returning to the world of the living, Izanagi birthed Amaterasu, the sun goddess, from his left eye and Tsukiyomi, the moon god, from his right eye.

VIRTUES

This mother goddess possessed the amazing power to form land out of a swirling chaos. She's also credited with having birthed all the deities who would be responsible for managing everything on earth, from the tallest mountains to the tiniest flowers. This part of her myth bears similarities to those of other creator goddesses who are revered in many cultures for having manifested the world we know.

Izanami, however, also brought death and destruction into the world as a result of her own death in childbirth, which suggests her roles as both creator and destroyer. Her dual powers make her one of the most awe-inspiring of the Japanese deities.

MANIFESTING HER POWER

What do you want to manifest in the world? Great works of art or architecture? Symphonies? Books? Are your goals of a domestic nature instead? Perhaps you seek to produce a happy, healthy family and provide a comfortable home for your children. Izanami can lend her creative power to any endeavor you pursue. She can help you find calm in the chaos. Ask the goddess to assist you in your objectives. To thank Izanami for her aid, prepare a flower arrangement in her honor. Your dedication to beauty reflects your dedication to this creator deity and to achieving your goal.

If you or someone you know is facing death—either a literal death or a figurative one—call on Izanami to help you handle the transition. As the goddess responsible for bringing death to earthlings, she can guide you in the passage from one state of being to another. If your transition involves letting go of an unwanted part of your life—a behavior, lifestyle, habit, attitude, or relationship, for instance—wash it away with the Shinto ritual of bathing. Soak in soothing, warm bathwater to which you've added purifying bath salts. Solicit the goddess's aid in helping you release what no longer serves you and ask her to guide you as you move into your new life.

KALI

"Kali is so called because She devours Kala (Time) and
then resumes Her own dark formlessness."

—Sir John Woodroffe, *The Garland of Letters*

HISTORY AND MYTHOLOGY

One of the most complex goddesses in the Hindu pantheon, Kali is associated with death and violence, but also with sexuality, fertility, and motherhood. Often she's depicted wearing a necklace of skulls and a skirt made of arms, sometimes holding a bloody knife to demonstrate her link to death and destruction. However, she's also viewed as an incarnation of Parvati, wife of the god Shiva, and she sometimes dances on him.

One myth says Kali was born from the head of the warrior goddess Durga during battle and became an angry, dark goddess who gobbled up demons. Kali didn't stop there, however; she then went after deities and humans whom she deemed guilty of wrongs. Shiva finally halted her reign of terror by throwing himself on the ground in front of her.

Another legend says Kali emerged from the dark skin Parvati shed, which might symbolize the separation of higher and lower aspects of Parvati. According to yet another story—which is also told of Durga—all the gods combined their energies to create a goddess who could destroy a troublesome demon. Kali came into being and quickly did away with the demon.

VIRTUES

In Sanskrit, Kali's name means "she who is black" or "she who is death," and artists usually present her as a wild, ferocious, dark-skinned female figure. Sometimes she sports numerous arms and many feet as well. In whatever form, she's a frightening being, although, to her followers, she

demonstrates a mother's fierce devotion and protection. Kali also represents primal, female power, as symbolized by the image of her dancing on the god Shiva. Her fearlessness is both a terrifying and an enviable quality, for most human beings fear a lot of things.

In some depictions, the goddess has three eyes that enable her to see past, present, and future. As the quote at the beginning of this section tells us, Kali transcends time, for in Hinduism, time and the physical world are illusions, or *maya*. She knows the great truths that can free humankind from the cycle of karma and reincarnation.

MANIFESTING HER POWER

Attachment—to people, things, ideas, possessions—keeps us bound to the wheel of birth, death, and rebirth. The destroyer goddess Kali cuts through our attachments, releasing us from bondage. Call upon her ruthless power if you're having trouble breaking an unwanted habit or need to get away from an unhealthy situation. Find or fashion something that symbolizes what you wish to eliminate (such as a cigarette if you want to stop smoking), then cut the symbol with a knife (or scissors) to sever your tie to it.

When you feel anxious or afraid, ask Kali to lend you her fierce determination. She can help you stand up to adversaries who may seem impossible to deal with by yourself. Ask her to put you in touch with the awesome, primal power that lies within you, the hidden courage at the core of your being. To raise Kali's energy, dance a spirited dance that expresses your desire to overcome your fears.

KUAN YIN

"One is meant to forgive, to forgive
and be compassionate."

—Hope Bradford, *Oracle of Compassion: The Living Word of Kuan Yin*

HISTORY AND MYTHOLOGY

The most revered goddess in the Chinese pantheon, Kuan Yin is sometimes thought of as the female equivalent of the Buddha. Her name is spelled various ways, including Quan Yin, Guanyin, and Kannon. However, not only the Chinese honor this beloved deity and bodhisattva—she holds a place of power and respect throughout Eastern Asia and is sacred in Taoism as well as Buddhism. *Kuan* means "earth" and *yin* refers to the feminine life force.

Mythology tells us that this merciful goddess heard the cries of humanity and, instead of entering heaven, she returned to earth. Here she will remain until all sentient beings have become enlightened, free from the cycle of birth, death, and reincarnation.

Many legends surround the goddess. One says Kuan Yin emerged from a pure white ray of light emanating from the eye of the Amitabha Buddha. According to another, a Chinese princess and Buddhist saint named Miao Shan, who lived about 700 B.C.E., was the embodiment of Kuan Yin. She wished to alleviate suffering due to illness, old age, and death, so instead of marrying, she became a nun. For nine years she lived on the sacred island P'u-t'o Shan where she rescued and healed shipwrecked mariners. Even today, she remains the patroness of seafarers. P'u-t'o became a holy destination for Kuan Yin's worshippers. Many temples, shrines, and monasteries exist there, where pilgrims claim to have seen miracles and visions of the goddess.

VIRTUES

The goddess of mercy and compassion, Kuan Yin upends a bottle or vase that contains the water of life, pouring it onto the earth to purify and heal all who abide here. Usually she wears a white robe and either sits on or holds a white lotus, representing purity. Sometimes she's depicted with a sheaf of rice or willow branch dripping nectar to show that she brings sustenance to the world. In some images she holds the pearls of illumination, signifying her enlightenment and all-encompassing peace. She's also portrayed riding a dolphin, a symbol of intuition, protection, and feminine power, or with a dragon, which represents wisdom and the primal creative force in the universe.

MANIFESTING HER POWER

Kuan Yin offers peace and blessings to all who call on her, especially women and children. The goddess of limitless mercy, she encourages you to nurture loving-kindness and compassion within you. She can help you become more gentle, patient, and forgiving toward yourself and others. When you feel yourself growing hard or judgmental, meditate on her example as you chant the mantra Om Mani Padme Hum to open your heart.

If an illness or disability is troubling you, ask Kuan Yin to ease your suffering or help you bear it with poise. Set a small statue of her in a place of honor and light a stick of incense to invite her spirit into the figurine. You can also float a white lotus blossom in a bowl of water as a gift to the goddess.

LAKSHMI

"I am one with the Power that created me. I am totally open and receptive to the abundant flow of prosperity that the Universe offers. All my needs and desires are met before I even ask."

—Louise Hay, *You Can Heal Your Life*

HISTORY AND MYTHOLOGY

Daughter of the Hindu mother goddess Durga, Lakshmi is thought of as the goddess of good luck and prosperity. This beloved deity's name derives from the Sanskrit word for "goal." Some images show her with golden coins flowing like water from her hands. Her blessings aren't only material, though—they include spiritual gifts such as peace and joy.

According to legend, Lakshmi came into the world as a full-grown female, floating on the foamy sea in a pink lotus-flower boat (similar to the birth of the Greek goddess Aphrodite). Everyone fell in love with her immediately and dressed her in finery and jewels. Wherever she went, good fortune and happiness prevailed.

Myth also portrays Lakshmi as a mother and fertility goddess who accompanied Lord Vishnu and represented his feminine counterpart. Some stories say the two deities reincarnate together throughout eternity to symbolize their undying love. Lakshmi personifies beauty, grace, and purity, too, and she often appears sitting or standing on a lotus blossom that signifies the unfolding of creative energy.

Lakshmi is a fond, familiar presence among homemakers and businesspeople alike, sought after and prayed to on a daily basis for her gifts of abundance. Ongoing devotion is said to strengthen the connection to the goddess and ensure her benevolence. Hindus celebrate her holiday in October or November, during which time people petition her for favors, offer her sweets, and string lights to welcome her into their homes.

VIRTUES

Like her mother, Durga, Lakshmi has several arms (usually four). She holds lotus blossoms, the symbol of creativity, in two of her hands. With her other hands she offers blessings and drops coins into the ocean from which life springs, as if sowing seeds for future growth and abundance.

This goddess of wealth usually wears red and golden clothing to signify her vitality and prosperity. Artists often depict her as beautiful and voluptuous to indicate her fertility, abundance, and enjoyment of pleasure and riches. Sometimes she's shown with her brother, the elephant-headed god Ganesh, who helps humans overcome obstacles. Together they work to improve conditions for people on earth and make success possible.

Unlike some of the frightening or awe-inspiring goddesses in the Hindu pantheon, Lakshmi is known as a "domestic goddess," gentle in nature and accessible to one and all. She brings harmony in daily life and inspires hope for better times. It's said that this goddess of all good things can show you the way to prosperity, greater happiness, a fulfilling marriage, and rewarding family life.

MANIFESTING HER POWER

To show Lakshmi the way to your home, affix tiny lights around your windows and doors. Or, place a single light or lantern near the entrance to your home. Invite her to visit you and bring good fortune of all kinds into your life. Offer her sweets to thank her for "sweetening" your days and nights.

For most of us, prosperity and abundance aren't one-time-only events, such as winning the lottery. The joy of an abundant life is an ongoing experience, nurtured on a daily basis in all we do. Establish a daily practice of honoring Lakshmi to keep the flow of blessings circulating. Pray to the goddess but also share the bounty you receive from her with others. Wear red or gold clothing to show your connection to her and to remind yourself that keeping your energy level high can help you attract good things.

LILITH

*"Lilith is not an enemy of womankind. She holds the
ancient fruit of knowledge, the secrets of our
deepest sexual nature, and She is willing to offer this fruit to us."*
—Daughter RavynStar, https://journeyingtothegoddess.wordpress.com

HISTORY AND MYTHOLOGY

One of the most misunderstood goddesses, Lilith frequently gets vilified in history and mythology as a demon or worse. Perhaps the first feminist, she's discussed in the Bible and in the Talmud, but also in ancient epics, including the millennias-old Sumerian *Epic of Gilgamesh*. Legend says Lilith was the first woman on earth, Adam's first wife, created at the same time he was. Described as independent and lusty (which may be why Christian and Jewish texts speak unfavorably of her), she's often connected with magic and witchcraft. Supposedly she demanded equality with her husband, sexually and otherwise, which caused problems in their relationship and resulted in Lilith either leaving or getting kicked out of Paradise.

One myth says Lilith—whom other stories say protected women and their babies—was punished for her audacity by being forced to give birth to a hundred demon children each day, who then died. Other legends say the night goddess Lilith shape-shifted into an owl and drank the blood of children while they slept. She's even said to have transformed herself into the serpent who convinced Eve to eat the apple and thus gain knowledge. (Was she causing trouble or trying to help Eve?) Still other tales link Lilith with the succubus and vampires.

VIRTUES

Passionate and sensual, independent and freedom-loving, this beautiful goddess terrified patriarchal religious cultures because she understood (and expressed) her sexual power. Furthermore, she defied the authority and demands of males, be they deities or mortals. She showed courage and confidence toward the "powers that be" and refused to be subservient to anyone, including her husband Adam.

Mythology tells us Lilith watched over and protected women and their infants during childbirth. Some stories say she nursed newborns, giving them extra strength that only a deity could provide.

According to legend, Lilith shape-shifted into an owl, symbol of wisdom. An ancient Sumerian relief sculpture portrays her with wings and bird feet. She supposedly took up residence in a sacred huluppu tree. In some cases, she's said to represent the tree's branches (parallels to the Kabbalah's Tree of Life) or to have lived as the tree's spirit/deva. Sometimes she's depicted with the head and torso of a woman and a serpent's lower body.

MANIFESTING HER POWER

Lilith can encourage you to stand up for your rights and beliefs. Do you feel unvalued? Are you being treated in an inequitable way? Perhaps you aren't being paid what you deserve or you're expected to put in more effort than your coworkers (or bosses) and you're not receiving the recognition you merit. From a tarot deck, choose the Empress card, which signifies feminine power, and meditate on it to gain perspective on how to handle your situation and claim your rightful authority.

Do you have questions, concerns, or anxiety related to your sexuality? Are your needs unfulfilled? Does your passionate spirit seem threatening to others? Ask Lilith to help you confront your fears and/or other people's judgment regarding your sensuality. Learn about snakes as age-old symbols of magic, knowledge, healing, transformation, and sexuality. Let Lilith show you how to express your sexuality fully. Read books or online articles about the sacred nature of sex that the ancients knew. Consider exploring the practice of sex magic and its creative power.

MA'AT

"One 'brings into being' Maat by the divine recitation of prayers in an unceasing effort where one listens to one another, where one acts one for the other. Thus social life and cosmic life intertwine: they are the reflection one of the other."
—Thierry Benderitter, www.osirisnet.net

HISTORY AND MYTHOLOGY

This Egyptian goddess had an awesome responsibility: she decided which souls ascended into the afterlife. To do this, she weighed a recently deceased person's soul (some myths say the heart) in the underworld, called Duat, using a set of cosmic scales. The soul could only get into the higher realm if it was lighter than the feather of truth. Those who didn't measure up became dinner for the lion deity Ammit. Thus, Ma'at became the ultimate arbiter of justice, order, morality, and balance. Her priests held positions within the judicial system and pharaohs proclaimed their allegiance to her (and the rules of law and order) by holding up a figurine of the goddess.

In her role as defender of order, Ma'at also kept the stars in place and controlled the cycle of the seasons. Her job included tending to the mortal realm, the natural world, and the entire cosmos. As such, she kept the universe from deteriorating into chaos.

Ma'at was one of the sun god Ra's daughters and the wife of Thoth, god of wisdom. In some legends, Shu, god of the wind/air who wore feathers (symbols of the air element and the intellect) in his hair, was her brother.

VIRTUES

Sometimes Ma'at is depicted as a woman with feathery wings; other times she wears a headdress of feathers or a single ostrich feather in her hair. Interestingly, the ostrich feather is equal in width on both sides of the central quill. Therefore, it signifies equality and balance. The feather became a symbol for the goddess and the hieroglyph for truth.

The goddess often holds a scepter to show her power and/or an ankh, symbol of life. In some images she sits or kneels on a stone platform that suggests stability and order are the foundations of existence.

For ancient Egyptians, Ma'at was a principle as well as a deity who outlined the moral way people, communities, and nations should conduct themselves. The goddess Ma'at, therefore, serves as the divine embodiment of the principle of order, balance, and justice. Today we see vestiges of this millennias-old belief system in the symbol of the scale used in connection with the legal profession. Both as a goddess and as an ideal system of organization and harmony, Ma'at points to the path of right living that promises salvation.

MANIFESTING HER POWER

If you're involved in a legal matter or are facing a decision of some kind, call upon Ma'at to help you receive justice. Carry a feather (preferably an ostrich feather) with you to a hearing, meeting, or other scenario where your "fate" will be determined. If you seek balance in your life, place the feather in a bowl of water and watch as it floats calmly. Think of Ma'at's fair and even temperament, and ask her to help you achieve the same.

Are you judging another person or assessing a situation in your life? Ask Ma'at to help you ascertain the truth and make a wise, just decision. Write a list of the pluses and minuses involved and weigh these to determine your next step. Try to respect the other person's position as well as your own, with the intention of finding an equitable resolution.

MAMA QUILLA

"When one starts thinking of the full moon as a common sight that will come again to one's eyes ad-infinitum, the value of life is diminished and life goes by uncherished."

—Roman Payne, *The Wanderess*

HISTORY AND MYTHOLOGY

The Incan moon goddess Mama Quilla (a.k.a., Mother Moon) was the wife and sister of the sun god Inti. She ranked third in the Incan pantheon, after Inti and Illapu, the god of thunder. Pachamama, the earth goddess, was her sister; however some myths say Mama Quilla gave birth to the earth and Pachamama.

Her children included Manco Capac and his sister/wife Mama Ocllo, who founded the Inca. One legend says Inti and Mama Quilla were unhappy with the primitive way humans conducted their lives, so they sent their son and daughter to earth to govern the people and establish civilization. The pair founded the sacred city of Cuzco and erected a temple where the Inca could worship Mama Quilla. They also taught the people to cultivate the land, fashion tools, weave fabric, and build houses.

Another legend says the Inca feared lunar eclipses, when they thought the moon goddess was being attacked by a wild animal. If the animal won and devoured the deity, the world would be plunged into darkness. Therefore, at these perilous times when the earth's shadow blotted out the moon's face, Mama Quilla's people made as much ruckus as possible in an attempt to scare off the animal.

Peru, where the Incan empire reigned, was once the world's largest producer of silver. According to mythology, when the goddess cried, her tears fell to earth and turned into silver.

VIRTUES

In Incan mythology, Mama Quilla governs women's menstrual and fertility cycles. The goddess is also considered a protector and defender of women, and a patroness of marriage. Unlike many other divine couples in the world's many cultures, she and her sun-god husband seemed to enjoy a happy marriage.

The Inca kept track of both solar and lunar cycles, and their calendars charted the moon's movements. Rituals, events, agriculture, and breeding times were aligned with the moon's phases. This understanding of the link between the heavenly bodies and earth placed Mama Quilla in the role of cosmic timekeeper.

Along with her husband, the goddess is also responsible for creating order and inspiring culture (through their children) among the ancient Peruvians. The moon and sun cycles symbolized by these deities depict the unwavering and eternal patterns of growth and decline on our planet.

MANIFESTING HER POWER

Ask Mama Quilla to guide you through the changes and challenges that women face at the different stages of their lives. This protector of women can offer guidance to girls embarking on womanhood, adult women during their childbearing years, and menopausal women. Today we may speak of the "man in the moon," but to the Inca, the moon wore a feminine face. Don a silver disc that represents the full moon to enhance your connection to Mama Quilla and the feminine force.

As the goddess of marriage, Mama Quilla can offer wisdom to women involved in primary relationships. She encourages you to see yourself and your partner as complements—neither is more important or dominant. The goddess also reminds you that relationships undergo cyclic ups and downs, and urges you to pay attention to these. Keep a journal of the moon's phases and notice how your emotions and interactions with your partner are influenced by the moon's movements.

MAMI WATA

"Mami Wata as the Divine African Mother/God/dess has been worshiped and celebrated around the world for thousands of years. From Egypt as 'Isis'…in Asia Minor (Ephesus) as 'Sibyl' (Cyeble), in Greece as Rhea, Hekate and Artemis, and in Rome as the great Magna Mater, Pravati, amongst her other holy names."

—Mama Zogbé, "Mami Wata: From Myth to Divine Reality"

HISTORY AND MYTHOLOGY

The name Mami Wata comes from the ancient Egyptian and Ethiopian words *mama* meaning "truth, wisdom" and *uat-ur* meaning "ocean water." Although commonly thought to be a single deity, Mami Wata actually refers to a pantheon of African water deities. According to some sources, Mami Wata brought divine law to earthlings—they were responsible for putting into place the social, economic, political, and moral structures that govern human life.

Mami Wata are generally viewed as benevolent and powerful divinities who govern natural cycles, including the Nile's overflow, agriculture, fishing, hunting, and so on. They're said to assist human beings physically and spiritually, and to provide food, shelter, protection, healing, and everything else we need to live on earth. In this respect, they share characteristics and responsibilities with other water deities. Legends sometimes link Mami Wata with wealth and say they bring prosperity to humans.

According to other stories, Mami Wata capture swimmers and boaters and shepherd them into other worlds—either the underwater realm or the spirit plane (which may mean the same thing, given that in mythology water often symbolizes spirituality, whereas psychology associates water with the subconscious and intuition). Those mortals who return to

earth may display a greater spiritual awareness or perhaps psychic ability as a result of their experiences with Mami Wata. They may also enjoy other benefits, such as financial abundance or physical attractiveness.

VIRTUES

Early depictions of Mami Wata often show them with the heads and torsos of humans and the lower bodies of fish or snakes, like mermaids. In later representations, Mami Wata morphed into a singular image of a voluptuous, long-haired African woman with a large snake—a symbol of wisdom and spiritual power—wrapped around her body.

As fertility goddesses, they watch over mothers and children. Some sources also credit them with guiding seers, mystics, and healers. Legends warn that Mami Wata aren't always gentle and generous, however. They can also be capricious and cantankerous. Mami Wata sometimes capture swimmers or sailors. If a person disobeys them, they may drown the errant follower or thrust him into a world of confusion, delirium, and disease.

MANIFESTING HER POWER

Humans, animals, and plants all need water to flourish. If you seek greater abundance and prosperity, call upon these benevolent water deities for assistance. They're known for their generosity, and they willingly provide bounty to those who honor them. To solicit their aid, place a birdbath in your yard or put out water for earth's creatures to quench their thirst.

If your life seems unsettled or your path unclear, Mami Wata can help you find direction and establish order. They can also teach you to flow with changes and adapt to cycles in life. Often this means accepting divine law instead of trying to force your will on a situation. To connect with Mami Wata, sit beside a stream or river and watch how the water continues flowing patiently along its course, wearing down obstacles over time.

MEDB

"Medb brings us the awareness of the intoxicating power of passion.
She personifies the passion of love and desire; of anger and war."
—Judith Shaw, "Medb, Celtic Sovereignty Goddess
of War and Fertility," https://feminismandreligion.com

HISTORY AND MYTHOLOGY

Also known as Maeve, the Celtic goddess Medb was said to have driven both mortal men and deities mad with desire. Her name means "intoxicating." According to legend, she had many lovers and at least four husbands, including King Conchobar, with whom she had seven sons, and King Aillil, who gave her three daughters. She's considered the Goddess of Connacht in western Ireland and legend says a man could only become king of Connacht if he engaged in "sacred marriage" with Medb.

In one well-known story about Medb, the goddess and her husband, Aillil, got into an argument over who owned more property. He pointed to his valuable magic bull named Finnbhennach (which some sources say originally belonged to Medb) as proof that he was richer. Medb decided to acquire another magic bull, Donn Cuailnge, from an Ulster man, and when she couldn't negotiate an agreement to purchase the bull, she organized an army to take the animal by force. When the men of Ulster caught sight of Medb, they were so overwhelmed by desire for her that they couldn't fight back. Only the Irish hero Cu Chulainn (who had some divine assistance from the Morrigan and the god Lugh) managed to resist the debilitating passion that disempowered the other soldiers.

Eventually, Medb and her lover, Fergus mac Roich, succeeded in capturing Donn Cuailnge and brought the bull back to Connacht. There he got into a fight with Aillil's bull, Finnbhennach, and killed him. However, Donn Cuailnge, too, died of wounds sustained in the fight.

VIRTUES

As a sign of her position as an earth goddess, Medb wore animals draped around her shoulders. Birds accompanied her wherever she went. Legend also links her with horses (an animal often associated with sexuality and passion). Some stories say she could outrun any horse. The mythic bull battle, too, holds sexual connotations, for bulls symbolize fertility. This feisty, independent goddess takes what she wants—men, bulls, etc. Known for her lusty nature and promiscuity, her fertility extended to the land.

Mythology depicts Medb as an irresistible beauty and a powerful goddess who could marshal one army and defeat another. However, she was also willful, proud, and egotistical. She alone decided who would reign over Connacht. Her competitiveness with her husband led to a conceited war based on greed and arrogance.

MANIFESTING HER POWER

The strong, determined Medb can help you increase your wealth or gain a position of power and respect. To connect with this earthy goddess, spend time observing and/or interacting with animals. Feed the birds. Ride horses. Support organizations that protect animal welfare. Read about spirit animals to learn which ones can assist you in achieving your goals.

If you wish to attract a lover or rekindle the flames in an existing relationship, ask Medb to share her sexual secrets with you. She can also help you achieve more equality and independence within a partnership. Acquire a figurine or other image of a bull, a symbol of virility, and display it in a place of honor as a gift to Medb. You might also want to dab a little musk essential oil on your pulse points to enhance your sex appeal—the heady scent can spark passion.

MESKHENET

"[T]here was a time when childbirth was possibly the most terrifying thing you could do in your life, and you were literally looking death in the face when you went ahead with it."

—Stephenie Meyer, *The Twilight Saga: The Official Illustrated Guide*

HISTORY AND MYTHOLOGY

The ancient Egyptians worshipped Meskhenet as the goddess of childbirth, a sort of cosmic midwife. Her name means "birthing place," and she safeguarded mother and child during the process of birth. Along with the protector god Khnum, she was said to drive away evil spirits that might harm the newborn and its mother.

Mythology tells us the goddess breathed Ka (part of the soul) into each child when it was born. As a visionary, Meskhenet could see the future and predict the baby's fate. She foretold which infants would grow up to become pharaohs. Thus, she was also considered a goddess of destiny.

Reputedly Meskhenet attended Queen Ahmose at the birth of her daughter, the noted Egyptian queen Hatshepsut, in 1473 B.C.E.—the story appears on the wall of the Mortuary Temple of Hatshepsut at Deir el-Bahri. Meskhenet also has connections to Ma'at, the goddess who weighs a deceased's soul to determine whether it's worthy to enter the afterlife. In the Hall of Judgment, Meskhenet bore witness to a person's character. Therefore, she not only provided protection at birth but also after the death of the physical body, when the soul was reborn and began its journey into the next world. These two seemingly opposing roles describe the ongoing cycle of birth, death, and rebirth.

VIRTUES

As divine midwife, Meskhenet is symbolized by the birthing brick: an earthenware block on which Egyptian women stood, squatted, or knelt to give birth. In the *Book of the Dead*, she's described as a brick with a human head. Her image often appeared on birthing bricks, along with scenes believed to have talismanic value. Paintings show her holding an ankh, symbol of life.

Because giving birth was a risky business in earlier times, Meskhenet was a revered and important deity who could decide life or death. With the goddess in attendance, Egyptian women felt more secure that they and their infants would survive. Mothers-to-be sought her favor and protection, but they also wanted to know what she could ascertain about their children's destinies. Meskhenet's ability to influence a child's fate with her breath gave the goddess awesome power over humankind.

MANIFESTING HER POWER

Are you curious about your destiny? Ask Meskhenet to reveal it to you. She may show it to you in a dream, during meditation, or in another way. Keep an open mind and watch for signs—record them in your journal. The goddess can also guide you in fulfilling the purpose for which you came to earth. The early Egyptians had knowledge of astrology, and you might like to consult with an astrologer to discover what the future holds.

If you or someone you know will soon give birth, invite Meskhenet to help keep mother and child safe. Ask her to use her divine skills to make everything go smoothly during birth. Consider giving the mother a necklace with an ankh on it to wear for good luck.

In her role as guardian of souls, Meskhenet can offer protection to someone who is about to pass out of this world and into the afterlife. Draw an ankh, the Egyptian hieroglyph for breath and life everlasting, on a piece of paper, then burn it to send a message to the goddess requesting her attendance at the person's transition.

THE MORRIGAN

"All is sinister now to see, / a cloud of blood moves over the sky, / the air is red with the blood of men, / and the battle women chant their song."
—H.R. Ellis Davidson, *Myths and Symbols in Pagan Europe*

HISTORY AND MYTHOLOGY

The name Morrigan means "great queen," but also "phantom queen." Sometimes she's described as the consort of the Irish god Dagda. This Celtic goddess of war and strife is part of the mythic Tuatha Dé Danann, a race of Irish deities who descended from the goddess Danu. It's said the Morrigan helped the Tuatha Dé Danann win two important battles at *Mag Tuireadh* in Ireland. In some stories she had two sisters, Badb and Macha, who were also war goddesses; however, other legends say these are aspects of the same goddess.

According to mythology, the Morrigan used magic as her weapon in battle. Instead of directly attacking a warrior, she deprived him of his power at a key stage in the fight, leaving him helpless and vulnerable. Assuming the form of a crow flying above the fray, she inspired either courage or fear in the soldiers. Thus, she chose who would live and who would die and determined the battle's outcome.

We find one example of this in the story of Cu Chulainn, son of the Celtic god Lugh. The Morrigan offered him her love but he rejected her. Some tales tell us the goddess then used her magic to bring him bad luck as revenge. Others say that she foretold his death in battle but didn't cause it. Reputedly, he saw her washing his bloody armor in a stream and knew his end was near. When he was killed, she shape-shifted into a crow and perched on his body.

VIRTUES

Because the Morrigan decided who would triumph in battle, and thus, influenced the destiny of nations, she's considered an arbiter of fate and linked with prophecy. She holds the power of life and death in her hands. She's also a divine guide who journeys between heaven and earth, bringing souls back home to the realm from which they came. Therefore, she represents the cycle of death and rebirth.

She specializes in binding magic—that is, she restricts someone's power and prevents him or her from achieving a desired goal or victory. Not surprisingly, she's often depicted as a crow (or raven), a bird we associate with both magic and death. Seeing a crow was sometimes believed to be an omen of impending death, and some legends connect the Morrigan with the Irish *bean sidhe* (banshee) who wailed just before a person died.

This shape-shifting goddess also showed herself as a beautiful woman, and sometimes as a horse, cow, or wolf. Some sources connect her with Morgan le Fey of the Arthurian legends, but this association is disputed.

MANIFESTING HER POWER

This goddess can assist you in making important decisions. Ask her to help you determine what you should hold on to and what you need to release from your life. Observe crows and pay attention to their behavior—they can provide clues to the Morrigan's instructions. For example, if a crow flies away it could mean freedom or rejecting a situation.

One of the Morrigan's jobs is to decide who lives and who dies. Some deaths are figurative, including the end of a friendship, leaving a job, or moving on to a different stage of life. If you feel this happening in your own life, request courage and insight from her. She can show you how to cope with loss. If someone you know has passed recently, ask the Morrigan for help in easing the pain of the person's passing and understanding that physical death is not the end. Wear black, not as a sign of mourning, but to connect with her and the mystery of the world beyond.

NEMESIS

"Nemesis…directs human affairs in such a manner as to restore the right proportions or equilibrium wherever it has been disturbed; she measures out happiness and unhappiness, and he who is blessed with too many or too frequent gifts of fortune, is visited by her with losses and sufferings, in order that he may become humble, and feel that there are bounds beyond which human happiness cannot proceed with safety."

—William Smith, *Dictionary of Greek and Roman Biography and Mythology*

HISTORY AND MYTHOLOGY

The Greek goddess of justice, revenge, and retribution, Nemesis had a reputation for coming down hard on mortals who don't honor the deities properly. In response to their arrogance (*hubris* in Greek) she could be ruthless. She also dealt sternly with humans who undeservedly received too much good fortune, as well as those who perpetrated suffering on others. In this way, Nemesis kept order on earth. No one could escape the divine retribution of this cosmic cop and judge. She was also called Adrasteia, meaning "inescapable."

One myth describes her treatment of the vain and disrespectful youth Narcissus. Nemesis showed him a sparkling pool of water where he saw his reflection staring back at him. Instantly he fell in love. So obsessed was he with his own image that he refused to leave and died beside the pool.

Another legend says Nemesis was the mother of Helen of Troy. In this story, the goddess took the form of a goose to escape the advances of Zeus, but he turned himself into a swan and mated with her. The consequence of that act was the Trojan War.

VIRTUES

Although she's often viewed as a wrathful goddess, Nemesis's job is to maintain balance on earth, curb excess, and make sure wrongdoers get their comeuppance. Her name means "dispenser of dues." You may see similarities between her and the Justice card in the tarot or the planet Saturn in astrology. Today, we use her name to refer to an unbeatable opponent, an avenger, or someone who calls your cards in the game of life and won't let you go until you pay your debts.

Artists sometimes depict Nemesis with a lash, scourge, reins, or sword, which she uses to check or discipline wayward mortals. Every society needs its taskmaster, and in Greek mythology, Nemesis fulfills this role.

MANIFESTING HER POWER

Petition Nemesis if you've suffered a recent or past injustice. Have you been treated unfairly by a boss? Has someone you love behaved in a disrespectful manner? Have other people received rewards and benefits they don't deserve, perhaps at your expense? Select the Justice card from a tarot deck and contemplate it while you ask Nemesis to set things right.

If you feel some part of your life has spun out of control—maybe you've maxed out your credit cards and are swimming in debt or you're eating too much unhealthy food—ask Nemesis to help you rein in your indulgences. Whenever things start getting out of balance, loosely wrap a piece of rope around your wrists for a few minutes and ask Nemesis to help you limit excesses.

If you're involved in a legal matter, Nemesis can be a formidable ally. Carry an image of her with you when you go to court, initiate a complaint, or engage in another proceeding. Ask her to ensure justice is done.

NEPHTHYS

*"A bridge of silver wings stretches from the dead ashes…
to the jeweled vision of a life started anew."*
—Aberjhani, *Journey Through the Power of the Rainbow*

HISTORY AND MYTHOLOGY

Daughter of the Egyptian earth god Geb and sky goddess Nut, and sister of the goddess Isis, Nephthys was the goddess of death and mourning, known as the Friend of the Dead. She accompanied the souls of the deceased into the afterlife, presided over funeral rites, and offered solace to loved ones left behind on earth. Whereas Isis was associated with birth, growth, light, and life in general, Nephthys represented the forces of decay, stagnation, and all that was dark or hidden. As goddess of the unseen, Nephthys became an ally of witches and magic workers who delved into the mysteries and tapped occult powers.

One of Egypt's oldest goddesses, Nephthys also served as a protector deity. She guarded the pharaohs throughout their lives and after they passed into the world beyond. Reputedly, she gave them the ability to see in the darkness. The goddess also accompanied her sister when Isis attended a birth—Isis functioned as the midwife while Nephthys offered protection to mother and child.

According to mythology, Isis's husband Osiris was killed and dismembered by her brother Set (also Nephthys's husband). Nephthys helped her sister retrieve the god's body parts and reconnect them again to bring Osiris back to life.

VIRTUES

Nephthys's expanded vision enables her to see what others can't—in the blackest night or in the shadowy, otherworldly realms beyond our physical one. Often she's depicted in the company of hawks or falcons, birds known for their keen sight, and some images show her with wings. She's also linked with the mythical phoenix that rose from the dead.

This goddess's transformative powers and her occult knowledge give her magical abilities. A cosmic shaman, she journeys through the different worlds and levels of reality, and can harness hidden forces in nature for her purposes. She also uses her magic to provide protection and healing, as well as for regeneration.

Some legends show Nephthys as a wise old woman beyond childbearing years. Others credit her as being the mother of the jackal-headed god Anpu (or Anubis, fathered by Osiris) who presided over the process of mummification.

MANIFESTING HER POWER

People who've lost loved ones or who are facing their own imminent deaths can turn to Nephthys for guidance and comfort. Ask her to help you understand that life doesn't end with the death of the body. View pictures of beautifully decorated Egyptian tombs, peruse the Egyptian *Book of the Dead*, and/or read books about the afterlife. Let Nephthys shepherd you through the process of grieving and ease the fear of death.

If you're experiencing a major life transformation—a symbolic death or ending—ask Nephthys to help you see beyond the darkness of your situation to the light at the other side. She'll offer protection and guidance during this difficult time. Display an image of the mythical phoenix to inspire you to rise from the ashes and soar again in a new way.

Seek this goddess during the darkest part of the night. Invite her to show you what you aren't seeing, what hides in the shadows, what lurks beneath the surface. If a hidden enemy or unseen situation threatens, ask Nephthys to protect you from harm. Close your eyes, touch the center of your forehead—site of the "third eye"—and ask her to strengthen your "second sight."

NIKE

"As long as we have faith in our own cause and an unconquerable will to win, victory will not be denied us."
—Winston Churchill

HISTORY AND MYTHOLOGY

The ancient Greeks considered Nike the goddess of victory. In Roman myth, she's called Victoria. She brought success in both battle and in athletic competitions, so it's no surprise the sporting goods company that bears her name chose her to represent it. Naturally, everyone loved Nike and wanted her on their side. As the daughter of Pallas and Styx, she had three siblings: Zelos (zeal), Kratos (strength), and Bia (force).

According to mythology, Zeus, the top god in the Greek pantheon, recruited these four sisters to participate in the war with the Titans for control of Mount Olympus. He appointed Nike to the position of head charioteer and legend says she flew above the battlefield rewarding soldiers for acts of skill and bravery. She's also said to have brought food and drink to warriors and purified them with incense. For her efforts, Zeus promised to protect and take care of Nike forever. She is sometimes pictured with Zeus on Olympus.

Greek legends associate (and sometimes muddle or overshadow) Nike with another war goddess, Athena. The 2,500-year-old Temple of Athena Nike still stands on the Acropolis in Athens. The most famous statue of the goddess, the Winged Victory of Samothrace, is in the Louvre in Paris, although the poor deity has lost her head. Today, Olympic medals feature a picture of Nike on them.

VIRTUES

According to myth, Nike possessed great speed and strength. Ancient Greeks believed she had the power to make them strong, invincible, and even immortal. Not only could she help them win battles and competitive games but she could also bring success in any endeavor.

The goddess is usually shown with feathered wings when she's alone, but wingless when in the company of her friend Athena. Artists sometimes depict Nike riding in a chariot. Often she wears a golden gown and bears symbols of victory, such as a palm branch, a trophy, a crown of laurel leaves to place on the champion's head, or a lyre on which to play a victory song.

MANIFESTING HER POWER

Whenever you must do battle with an adversary—whether in a physical fight, on the playing field, or in the boardroom—ask Nike to accompany you and bring you success. She's the ideal deity to befriend if you're in the military. Carry or wear a piece of bloodstone as ancient Greek soldiers did for protection in combat.

Known as a goddess of speed and strength, Nike can help you accomplish a difficult task. Call on her when you're facing a tight deadline and must work extra hard to finish a job on time. Keep a feather nearby as a token of the winged goddess. With her assistance, you'll win praise and respect for your efforts.

Nike can also help with physical fitness. While exercising, call on Nike to give you strength and stamina. When you feel yourself getting winded, remember Nike's athletic prowess and ask her to share her vitality with you. Let the sweat on your brow remind you of your own physical capabilities.

Invite Nike to join you in celebrating a victory. Play music and dance. Wear a crown of laurel leaves. Toast yourself and the deity. Light incense to thank the goddess for helping you to achieve your success.

NUT

"Have you ever stood under a star…and felt the earth move under your feet?"
—Michael Poeltl, *The Judas Syndrome*

HISTORY AND MYTHOLOGY

Goddess of the sky and all the celestial bodies, Nut is one of the earliest deities in the Egyptian pantheon. According to myth, she swallowed the sun each evening, and it then moved through her body during the night and was reborn every morning. She was the daughter of Shu, the god of air, and Tefnut, goddess of rain/moisture. Nut and her husband (also her brother), Geb, god of the earth, had five children together: Isis and her husband Osiris, Nephthys and her husband Set, and Horus the Elder.

Another legend says that when Ra, the sun god, found out Nut was going to give birth, he feared his power might be usurped. He decreed that she would not have a child on any day of the year. (At the time, the Egyptian year had only 360 days.) Thoth, god of wisdom, devised a plan, however. He played a gambling game with the moon god, Khonsu, and whenever Khonsu lost a round, he had to give up some of his light. Not surprisingly, the wise Thoth won often, and soon he had enough light to create five new days. Because these days weren't part of the original year, Nut was able to birth one child on each day.

VIRTUES

Often Nut is depicted as a woman with her hands and feet on the ground—one at each of the compass directions: north, south, east, and west—symbolizing the four pillars that hold up the sky. Her body arches over Geb, representing the heavens hovering over her husband, the earth. Legend says that when Shu placed Nut above Geb, the chaos in the world ended. Consequently, she signifies order and a balanced relationship between our planet and the rest of the cosmos.

Her responsibility for creating day and night gives her a mother-creator aspect too. Her regenerative ability makes her a powerful deity indeed.

The Egyptians believed that when people died, Nut took their souls into her realm. Therefore, she was also seen as a protector of the dead. Her image as the nighttime sky, her dark-blue body spangled with stars, was often painted on the ceilings of tombs and the inside lids of sarcophagi to aid the dead on their journey into the afterlife.

MANIFESTING HER POWER

If your life seems unbalanced or chaotic, Nut's energy can help bring order into your world. The sky remains in its place throughout eternity, and its relationship to the earth is unchanged. Day follows night. Listen for a message from her upon awakening in the morning. Go outside at night and gaze up at the sky with its myriad stars. Sense your connection to both the sky and the earth. Feel Nut's majesty and peace as she shows you how to restore harmony.

In her role as protector of the dead, Nut can offer solace to those who've lost loved ones. Call on her to give you insight into the world beyond this one. At sunset, light a dark blue candle in her honor and say prayers by candlelight. At dawn, watch the sun rise and draw comfort from knowing that there is consistency and continuity in the universe. Let the goddess reveal the inherent order in the cycle of life, death, and rebirth.

ODUDUA

"A family is like a forest, when you are outside it is dense, when you are inside you see that each tree has its place."

—African proverb

HISTORY AND MYTHOLOGY

Worshipped by the Yoruba in Nigeria and other parts of Africa, the earth goddess Odudua is the sister of the sky god Olorun. Together the two deities personify earth and heaven. According to myth, Odudua is the mother of all that exists on earth—she formed our planet from her primal energy. Odudua (a.k.a., Odua) married Obatala, god of harmony, and gave birth to the beautiful water goddess Yemaya.

When it becomes necessary to protect the earth or her people, legend says Odudua shifts into warrior mode. At such times she may stir up destructive weather patterns or natural disruptions such as earthquakes to thwart an enemy.

Also a goddess of love, Odudua reputedly had many mates. One story says she took an interest in a handsome hunter, a mortal, and they engaged in a passionate affair. After a few weeks they parted company, but the goddess promised to protect him always and to take care of everyone who came to the place where they had lived together happily. A community soon arose in that spot and developed into the city of Ado-Ekiti in southwestern Nigeria.

VIRTUES

Odudua translates as "black one" and artists usually portray the goddess as a vibrant, handsome woman with ebony-colored skin, adorned with jewelry, sometimes wearing an ornate cap on her head. Mother-earth

goddesses everywhere watch over and protect women and children, and Odudua is no exception. Not only is she a patron of mothers but she also supports and nurtures family life in general. Along with her husband Obatala, she endeavors to bring peace and unity to her people. Maintaining harmony within the larger community is also Odudua's responsibility. This amiable deity just wants everyone to be happy.

Like earth goddesses in other cultures, Odudua governs fertility, abundance, and creativity in many forms. She's responsible for the fruitfulness of the land as well as human reproduction. Her primal energy, from which she formed our planet, continues to nourish all of earth's inhabitants to this day.

MANIFESTING HER POWER

When disagreements, ego battles, or everyday stresses upset your family life, turn to Odudua for guidance. She can show you the importance of restoring unity and order, and encourage you to nurture the good things that hold you together as a clan. Myths often connect Odudua and her peace-loving husband with the calabash (a type of gourd with a hard skin that can be made into a dipper-like utensil). Make a soup for your family members and serve each other with a gourd ladle. The act of sharing this dish is a sign of coming together and nourishing one another.

If you desire greater prosperity or if money seems to go out faster than it comes in, tap into Odudua's fertile nature. Acquire a black stone—jet, onyx, or obsidian, for instance—and carry it in your purse or pocket. If you prefer, you can bury the stone just outside the door to your home to stabilize your resources. Or, take the stone to work and set it on your desk—or wherever you perform your job—to attract wealth.

OSHUN

*"I am the honey-sweet voice of the waters. I am the flowing of
a woman's skirts as she dances her life."*
—Thalia Took, creator of *The Goddess Oracle Deck*

HISTORY AND MYTHOLOGY

Daughter (some sources say sister) of the sea goddess Yemaya and the god Obatala, the African goddess Oshun lives in the Ogun River in Nigeria. However, legends say you can find her in all streams, rivers, lakes, and ponds around the world. Like many water deities, she represents fertility, prosperity, nourishment, and healing. Best known as a love goddess, she's also the beloved protector and provider of the Yoruba people. She cares for the poor, the sick, and all orphans, as well as the fish and birds. This sweet-tempered and kindhearted river goddess is revered for her generosity toward her people. She brings joy to one and all and represents love in its myriad forms: romantic, sexual, maternal, creative, humanitarian, and spiritual. It's said that only injustice toward her followers and lack of reverence for the deities will rouse her anger.

Myths also credit her with teaching agriculture, music, dance, and the art of divination. A festival held each year in July and August at the Osun-Osogbo Sacred Grove in Nigeria honors this benevolent river goddess.

VIRTUES

Some images of Oshun present her as a mermaid, with the torso of a beautiful woman and the tail of a fish. Others depict her as a lovely, sensual, and charismatic young human female. Like love goddesses everywhere, Oshun is irresistibly beautiful and desirable. She tends to be rather vain, indulgent, and superficial, though, and can't help admiring herself in the reflecting surface of a freshwater pool.

She's fascinated by pretty, shiny things—artists often show this luxury-loving goddess decked out in sumptuous jewelry and holding a mirror. Legend says she's a big fan of perfume too—particularly lush, sensual fragrances like amber, patchouli, and frankincense. Sweet foods of all kinds delight her, especially honey.

Oshun possesses the gifts of divination and spellcasting, which she learned from her father. She's also associated with magic and witchcraft. As a love goddess, naturally she likes casting love spells best.

MANIFESTING HER POWER

Seek Oshun's assistance if you want to attract a new romantic partner or wish to increase the love and passion in an existing relationship. She can teach you her beauty secrets and give you tips for enhancing your sensuality. Let her guide you in the seductive art of aromatherapy. Anoint yourself with a favorite essential oil, and then pour a few drops of the oil into a body of fresh water as an offering to the goddess.

Ask Oshun to help you become more prosperous. Known for her generosity and creative power, she can show you how to attract abundance of all kinds. Follow her example and share your good fortune with others, instead of hoarding it all yourself. To keep the flow of prosperity coming, donate some of your riches to charity, perhaps to aid orphans. Learn from Oshun's generosity by helping others whenever you can. This may mean simply listening to a friend talk about her problems, or volunteering at your local homeless shelter.

Do you want to know what the future holds? Gaze into a still, clear pool of water (or a magic mirror) and invite Oshun to show you what lies beyond your ordinary range of vision.

OSTARA

"Ostara, Eástre seems therefore to have been the divinity of the radiant dawn, of upspringing light, a spectacle that brings joy and blessing, whose meaning could be easily adapted by the resurrection-day of the Christian's God."

—Jacob Grimm, *Deutsche Mythologie*

HISTORY AND MYTHOLOGY

The word *Easter* derives from the name of the Germanic goddess Ostara (or Eostre), and Western culture has adopted some elements of her mythology into the Christian holiday, specifically rabbits and eggs, both symbols of fertility. In the Northern Hemisphere, spring is the season when the earth blossoms, bringing forth new plant and animal life. Pagans honor the goddess Ostara on the spring equinox (around March 21, the first day of the astrological year).

According to legend, a rabbit laid some sacred eggs and decorated them as a gift for the fertility goddess Ostara. Ostara liked the beautiful eggs so much that she asked the rabbit to share them with everyone throughout the world. Ukrainian folk art gives us some of the best examples of the ritual of egg decoration. Traditionally, people painted eggs to provide protection and healing. They then carried the pretty eggs as talismans and exchanged them as gifts.

VIRTUES

As goddess of the dawn, Ostara represents new life, hope, opportunity, and awakening. Symbolically, sunrise offers not only opportunity on the horizon, but also a fresh perspective in the clean, clear light that unfolds at daybreak before the day's complications and problems crop up. Therefore, Ostara brings clarity as well as a chance to begin anew.

Usually she's depicted as a lovely young woman, the maiden aspect of the Triple Goddess, in her role as goddess of springtime. Although she's connected with fertility and creativity, she's not a mother deity. Rather, her youth signifies innocence, potential, optimism, and vitality. She's often shown wearing flowers in her hair or around her neck. Some legends say she could shape-shift into a rabbit. Like spring itself, Ostara brings joy into the world, and, like the return of warm weather after winter's harshness, she represents resurrection and rebirth.

MANIFESTING HER POWER

The spring equinox marks the first day of spring (in the Northern Hemisphere) and the start of the busy planting season in agrarian cultures. This holiday is a fertility festival and a time for planting seeds, literally or figuratively. To engage Ostara, start to sow "seeds" that you want to bear fruit in the coming months. This is an ideal time to launch new career ventures, move to a new home, or begin a new relationship. As the new year begins, tap the energy of the goddess to help you birth a new endeavor. Write a wish on a piece of paper, then put it in a flowerpot and fill the pot with soil. Plant flowers and dedicate them to the goddess. Ask her to grant your wish in return.

If you've been going through a difficult period, call upon Ostara to bring hope and joy into your life. According to an old custom, people who were ill carried an egg with them for a day and a night, then buried the egg (and symbolically the illness) the following dawn. Bury an egg to represent letting go of your problems.

OYA

"Oya-Yansa is the Queen of the Winds of change. She is feared by many people because She brings about sudden structural change in people and things. Oya does not just rearrange the furniture in the house—She knocks the building to the ground and blows away the floor tiles."
—Luisah Teish, *Jambalaya*

HISTORY AND MYTHOLOGY

In Yoruba mythology, Oya is the goddess of storms. Her name translates as "she who tore." Legend has it that lightning bolts, thrown by her brother/husband Shango, appear to rip the sky during her thunderstorms. She whips up the winds and hurls them across the landscape and roils the waters until they overflow the shores and flood the land. Mythology says she lives in the Niger River (in Nigeria), and she's the older sister of the water goddesses Oshun and Yemaya.

As goddess of chaos, Oya refuses to be contained or regulated. She brings life-altering transformations, the greatest being birth and death. She's often portrayed as the guardian who stands at the threshold between the realms of the living and the dead. By extension, she governs cemeteries, funeral rites, and other things related to death.

The Yoruba both revere and fear the irrepressible Oya. There's nothing subtle about her. In the pursuit of justice and fairness, the goddess reveals truth—often in a sudden blaze of light. However, this may come as a shock, with upsetting consequences. Astrologers might connect her with the zodiac sign Aquarius and tarotists with the Death card of the Major Arcana.

VIRTUES

Legend portrays Oya as impatient, tempestuous, passionate, fiercely independent, and totally unpredictable. She's a wild, fearless warrior goddess who wreaks havoc in your life. The sudden, often unexpected changes she instigates aren't just temporary adjustments—they're major inner and outer transformations, and your life will never be the same after Oya rampages through it.

Despite the destruction the goddess leaves in her wake, the changes she instigates are usually for the better. Sometimes artists show her sweeping away debris with her cosmic broom. After the storm, she cleanses and renews.

Oya's familiarity with death and rebirth and the world beyond gives her psychic power. She can see the future and communicate with spirits. Adept in the magical arts, she understands how to concoct and use spells of all kinds. Thus, she's a patron of witches and other magic workers.

MANIFESTING HER POWER

When you're in the midst of a life-altering transformation, ask Oya to help you weather the changes and chaotic situations you're experiencing. During a storm, listen to her voice in the wind. Watch for revelation in the brilliant flash of lightning. Pay attention to the insights sparked by your intuition. Oya can guide you through turmoil and upheaval—the dark night of the soul—and show you the light at the end of the tunnel.

If you feel trapped or unmotivated, ask Oya to help stir up energy and change. With a broom, sweep away clutter and dust as a symbolic gesture of removing the old "stuff" that has held you back. Remember that no one can change your life but you, though Oya can certainly help get things moving.

Do you need to know the truth about something? Are you seeking fairness, justice, or vindication? Enlist the support of this warrior goddess as you uncover secrets and lies and bring them into the light. At the darkest hour just before dawn, light a white candle in Oya's honor. Gaze into the flame as you express your intention to her. Don't underestimate her power—call upon her with utmost caution and reverence, and be willing to roll with the punches that may result from your pursuit.

PACHAMAMA

"Nature always wears the colors of the spirit."
—Ralph Waldo Emerson, "Nature"

HISTORY AND MYTHOLOGY

The Incan earth goddess Pachamama, like earth deities in other cultures, is said to govern the fertility of our planet, the planting and harvest seasons, and all things related to earth's productivity. She also presides over animals and humans—in short, the Inca believed she brought the world we know into being and continues to oversee it.

Legend says Pachamama took up residence under the Andes Mountains, where she lived as a dragon. Artists sometimes depict her as part woman, part mountain. During the planting season, Incan women walked through the fields sprinkling cornmeal on the ground and saying prayers to the goddess, requesting her beneficence and bounty. When her people didn't pay Pachamama the respect she deserved, she supposedly shivered, causing earthquakes to occur across the land. Inti, the sun god, and Mama Quilla, the moon goddess, were her children (although Inti is also described in myth as her husband).

In August, at the beginning of the planting season, Peruvians and other indigenous people of the Andes still celebrate a festival known as Martes de Challa to honor Pachamama. Her people prepare an abundant feast and bury food in the ground to show their gratitude for her generosity and to petition the goddess for continued prosperity. Coca leaves, herbs, incense, and other substances are often burned as offerings to Pachamama.

VIRTUES

The mother-earth goddess Pachamama has the awesome responsibility of sustaining life on planet earth. A benevolent deity, she's the personification of our planet, and she lovingly cares for all that she's created in the manifest world. She generates fertility in the land, in animals, and in human beings. Everything comes from and depends on her.

Untamed, sometimes destructive, yet always caring, Pachamama enables us to reconnect with the "wild" part of ourselves. The goddess teaches humankind to respect the land, to appreciate its beauty, and to live in harmony with nature. Those who follow her wise counsel can reap prosperity and blessings of all kinds. By drawing on the earth's nurturing and restorative powers—Pachamama's powers—we can find security, stability, and contentment in our world.

MANIFESTING HER POWER

Stress is rampant in our modern world, in part because we've lost our connection to Mother Earth and are no longer in balance with nature. To renew your link with Pachamama, sit on the ground and try to sense her life-giving energy flowing into your body through your root chakra (at the base of your spine). Close your eyes and take several deep breaths, drawing in her nourishment with each inhalation. With each exhalation, release stress into the earth for Pachamama to neutralize.

This nurturing mother-goddess can help you improve your health and vitality. Go for regular walks in nature, without talking or texting or listening to music. Pay attention to your surroundings—the landscape and life forms that inhabit it. Listen to the wind, leaves crunching under your feet, birdsong, etc. Give thanks to the earth that is your home.

Is your life too hectic? Are you torn in many directions so that you don't feel you accomplish much no matter how hard you try? Ask Pachamama to show you how to get centered and renew your energy rather than burn out. Acquire a grounding stone—onyx, hematite, and black tourmaline are good choices—and meditate while holding it to encourage stability and focus.

PARVATI

"She [Parvati] is a wonderful affirmation that there are
no limits to what a woman can do when she uses
her spiritual energy in the pursuit of any goal she chooses."
—Sharon Turnbull, www.goddessgift.com

HISTORY AND MYTHOLOGY

Hindu mythology considers Parvati a goddess of love and peace. The second wife of Lord Shiva, god of destruction, she was daughter of the Lord of the Mountains. In fact, her name means "mountain."

According to one legend, Parvati saved the world from destruction by demons. The great Shiva had withdrawn to a cave to meditate and grieve the death of his first wife. Without him in charge, evil spirits wreaked havoc on the land. At the request of the other deities, Shakti (the feminine force in the universe) took the form of Parvati and set out to win over Shiva. Even though he rejected her, Parvati loved him. Each day she brought him food and flowers and cleaned his cave. She even became an ascetic herself, devoted to yoga and meditation.

Finally Brahma, the top deity, took note of her dedication and offered to help her. She asked him to make her dark skin light, which he did. Some versions of the legend say the goddess Kali was created from the dark skin Parvati shed. When Shiva saw the transformed goddess, he fell in love with her, abandoned the cave, and went with her to live again on the sacred mountain Kailash at the heart of the universe. Parvati collected some of Shiva's essence and planted it in the earth. The "seed" grew into the god Kartikeya, who defeated the demons and restored peace.

VIRTUES

Gentle and peace-loving, Parvati was unwavering in her devotion to Shiva and to her goal of bringing peace to the world. She's respected for her compassion, patience, and selflessness, as well as her great love and affection. During her time as an ascetic, the goddess gained abundant wisdom and power, which enabled her to guide Shiva and bring out the best in him. Thus, she's considered a goddess of marriage as well as an inspired counselor who, alongside Shiva, ruled with kindness.

Although the goddess was best known for her calm, patient, and caring nature, Parvati could also be strong and assertive—a side she showed when she determined to overcome the demons. Through her combination of serenity and strength, she also managed to temper Shiva's violence and channel it into productive endeavors.

Sometimes she's shown with two hands, holding a blue lotus blossom in one of them. At other times she has four hands, with two positioned in sacred mudras. Parvati is said to have 108 names and ten aspects expressed as other goddesses, including Kali and Tara.

MANIFESTING HER POWER

As a goddess of love and marriage, Parvati can give strength and perseverance to people who are involved in challenging relationships. She'll show you how to be patient and compassionate, even toward difficult mates, while remaining true to yourself. Float a lotus blossom in a bowl of water to honor her. Ask the goddess to help you deal with disappointments in love and to continue on, holding firmly to your self-worth instead of letting someone else's opinion or bad behavior disempower you.

If you're following a spiritual path, Parvati can guide you through the rigors you encounter along the way. She'll lend you determination and help you release ego demands, attachments, and the desire for luxury in your pursuit of wisdom. During meditation, position your hands in sacred mudras to connect with the goddess and higher knowledge.

PELE

"[A] good love is one that…sets you ablaze, makes you burn through
the skies and ignite the night like a phoenix; the kind that
cuts you loose like a wildfire and you can't stop running simply
because you keep on burning everything that you touch!"
—C. Joybell C., author

HISTORY AND MYTHOLOGY

As the goddess of fire in Hawaiian and Polynesian mythology, Pele shows herself and her immense power through volcanoes and lightning. Both a creator and a destroyer deity, she caused new islands to emerge from the sea and wiped out lands with molten lava flows. Legend says she originated in Tahiti (or perhaps a nonphysical place called Kuaihelani), the daughter of the earth goddess Haumea and the sky god Kane Milohai.

One story tells us Pele's parents banished her from her south sea home after she seduced the husband of her older sister, the sea goddess Namaka. Another says Pele set Tahiti on fire, which understandably upset everyone. Pele traveled across the sea to Hawaii (which was only a tiny island), carrying her not-yet-born younger sister Hi'iaka in an egg. When Pele arrived at her destination, Namaka tried to kill her. The fire goddess survived and spent her time building volcanoes that formed the various islands. She eventually made her home in the Kilauea volcano on the "Big Island," Hawaii, where it's said she still lives today.

According to some legends, Pele was initially a mortal and a firebrand. Only after her physical death was she promoted to goddess.

VIRTUES

The tempestuous goddess Pele is best known for creating the Hawaiian Islands. Famous for her violent temper, Pele often regretted the results of her rages and set about creating something of beauty in the wake of the destruction she'd brought. One myth credits Pele with producing Hawaii's exquisite flowers as a result of her clashes with the snow goddesses who lived on the islands' mountain peaks. Another says Pele killed a mortal man she desired when he shunned her, and then she turned him into a lovely flowering tree.

Passionate, and some might say promiscuous, Pele had many lovers, both human and divine. She pursued what she wanted and never let an adversary intimidate her. Thus, she represents powerful emotion, desire, willfulness, and daring. Her drive to achieve her aims sometimes brought disaster, but also greatness, as was the case for many creator-destroyer deities. On a lighter note, Pele loves to dance and supposedly invented the hula.

MANIFESTING HER POWER

Pele shows you how to marshal your courage, desire, and willpower to achieve whatever you want. This feisty goddess can help you overcome fears or hesitations that may be keeping you from accomplishing your objectives. Are you a naturally cautious or shy person? Ask Pele to fire up your vitality so you can take on opponents, either on the playing field or in the boardroom. Dance a hula and feel the power of the creative feminine rejoicing in your body. You can also symbolically ignite your inner fire by using hot peppers or spices when you cook.

Do you need to get rid of something in your life so something new can emerge? Call upon Pele to guide you through the process of destruction and creation. On a piece of paper, write what you wish to eliminate. On another piece of paper, write what you wish to create. Light a fire in a fireplace, barbecue grill, or cauldron and drop the first piece of paper in it to release the old. When it has finished burning, drop the second piece of paper into the flames to spark something new.

PERSEPHONE

*"I warned you, daughter. This scoundrel Hades is no good.
You could've married the god of doctors or the
god of lawyers, but noooo. You had to eat the pomegranate."*

—Rick Riordan, *The Last Olympian*

HISTORY AND MYTHOLOGY

The only daughter of Demeter and Zeus, the Greek goddess Persephone has two faces: that of the youthful maiden (or Kore) and that of the Queen of the Underworld. The Romans knew her as Proserpina or Cora.

In the most famous myth about her, the young goddess went out to pick flowers. When she plucked a narcissus, Hades burst out of the ground and dragged Persephone back to the underworld to be his unwilling bride. Her broken-hearted mother, Demeter, convinced Zeus to intervene, and the god dispatched the messenger god Hermes to bring his daughter back. There was a problem, however. While in the underworld, Persephone had eaten some pomegranate seeds. As a result, she couldn't completely sever her tie to Hades and his realm.

A bargain was negotiated. Persephone would spend part of the year above ground and part below. While Persephone resided with her mother, the Goddess of Grain who made everything grow, the earth flourished. When Persephone descended to the underworld, Demeter destroyed the crops.

According to another legend, both Persephone and Aphrodite loved the handsome Greek youth Adonis. Zeus had to step in and work out a deal between the two goddesses to end their dispute. He ruled that Adonis would spend one-third of the year with Persephone and one-third with Aphrodite; the other third he was free to do as he pleased.

VIRTUES

Persephone's story represents the cycle of birth, death, and rebirth. As Kore, she's the beautiful young goddess of springtime. As Queen of the Underworld, she watches over the dead and guides mortals (including Odysseus) as well as deities on sojourns into the underworld.

Mythology depicts Persephone as a rather passive goddess, gentle, naive, and unassuming. She doesn't take charge of her own destiny; instead, things happen to her and decisions are made for her. Therefore, she represents the receptive or yin principle. Additionally, she's linked with compromise because the best-known legends about her revolve around a deal that must be struck in order to resolve a conflict. As a result of her experiences, however, she grows from a demure maiden into a powerful queen, suggesting she has a deeper, hidden layer to her psyche.

MANIFESTING HER POWER

Ask Persephone to be your guide as you explore the hidden realms of your psyche—she can serve as your divine therapist. If you're facing a difficult time, the so-called "dark night of the soul," ask her to give you the strength to accept what you can't change and to grow from the experience. Persephone can also help you guide others through challenges. Offer her a vase of narcissus as a thank-you gift.

As Queen of the Underworld, the goddess can help you face a literal or figurative death courageously. If you're interested in revisiting your past lives, she's the perfect deity to accompany you on the journey. Eat a pomegranate to understand Persephone's experience of death and rebirth.

RAINBOW SERPENT

"Before our globe had become egg-shaped or round it was a long trail of cosmic dust or fire-mist, moving and writhing like a serpent."
—Manly Palmer Hall, *The Secret Teachings of All Ages*

HISTORY AND MYTHOLOGY

According to the mythology and ancient rock art of the aboriginal people of Australia, a deity known as the Rainbow Serpent created the earth and everything on it. Some stories say Rainbow Serpent was a god, but others describe her as a goddess. Still others speak of a female serpent Yingarna who brought forth the earth and a male serpent Ngalyod who shaped it. The goddess is said to abide in waterholes, which the Aborigines credit with having the power of fertility. Supposedly a woman can become pregnant simply by dipping her feet in a waterhole. When a rainbow appears in the sky, it's a sign the goddess is going from one waterhole to another.

Many legends exist about Rainbow Serpent. One tells us the deity awoke from the Dreamtime (the world inhabited by ancestors, deities, and other supernatural beings) and roamed the planet, leaving winding indentions and hollows in the ground. These she filled with water, and they became rivers, lakes, and oceans. Next, she fashioned plants and woke up the animals that had been sleeping in the Dreamtime. The goddess established laws so the animals could live together harmoniously, but some disobeyed her and she turned them into rocks. She transformed some who followed her rules into humans. At times, when Rainbow Serpent becomes displeased with her earthly children, she punishes them with torrential rainstorms and floods.

VIRTUES

Rock art depicts Rainbow Serpent as a colorful amalgam of several Australian creatures, frequently with a kangaroo's head, a python's body, and a crocodile's tail. Like creator-deities in myriad traditions, she's responsible for the fertility of the land as well as its inhabitants. She governs women's reproductive cycles and the cycle of the seasons.

Rainbow Serpent's fertility is based in the life-giving nature of water, for the goddess has dominion over all bodies of water, as well as rain—and, of course, rainbows. Without her, nothing could exist. And, like many creator-goddesses, she also has a destructive side.

In many cultures snakes are associated with magic. Rainbow snakes, according to legend, reputedly can take up residence in a person's body and give him or her special powers. However, the snakes can also cause illness and death by leaving "rainbows" inside a human being—another example of Rainbow Serpent's dual nature as a deity who both gives and takes away.

MANIFESTING HER POWER

Creative people can draw upon Rainbow Serpent's powers to inspire imagination and insights. Artists, in particular, may find the colorful deity appealing. The Aborigines link Rainbow Serpent with quartz crystals, perhaps because, like prisms, they break light into rainbow colors. Acquire a quartz crystal and set it on a sunny windowsill while you're working to spark your creativity.

If you wish to become pregnant, solicit the aid of Rainbow Serpent. Swim, wade, or sit beside a body of water and feel the fertile energy of the goddess within you. A woman may also want to carry a shell to symbolize the womb and life-giving water; a man could carry a small representation of a snake as a phallic symbol.

RHEA

"Upon the Mother depend the winds, the ocean, the whole earth beneath the snowy seat of Olympus."

—Apollonius of Rhodes, *Argonautica*

HISTORY AND MYTHOLOGY

The daughter of Gaia (goddess of the earth) and Ouranos (god of the sky), the Greek goddess Rhea was called the Mother of Gods and known as Ops in Roman mythology. As her moniker suggests, Rhea produced several of the most important gods and goddesses in the Greek pantheon: Zeus, Hera, Demeter, Poseidon, Hades, and Hestia. Her husband, Cronus, however, feared one of his offspring would overthrow him (as he'd done to his own father), so as each child was born he quickly devoured it.

Tired of having her children eaten, Rhea tricked Cronus when Zeus (the youngest) was born. She hid her baby in a cave in Crete where her mother, Gaia, took care of him, and gave her husband a stone wrapped in a blanket instead. Cronus swallowed the stone, then choked and vomited up Zeus's five siblings.

According to other legends, this mother goddess cared for the young wine god Dionysius and protected him from the wrath of Zeus's jealous wife Hera. Some stories tell us Rhea sewed the god back together after he'd been ripped to pieces by the Titans (under Hera's direction). Rhea is also said to have served as midwife at the birth of the sun god Apollo. And when Demeter sunk into terrible grief after the abduction of her daughter Persephone, Rhea urged her fellow goddess not to abandon Mount Olympus and destroy humankind.

VIRTUES

Rhea's name means "flow" and "ease," and, not surprisingly, she was responsible for making things go smoothly. She represents the continuous movement of seasons, generations, the tides, and time in general. As a fertility goddess, she's also linked with the cycle of women's menstrual flows.

Legend connects Rhea with lions. Sometimes she's depicted on a throne with lions as her attendants, sometimes riding in a chariot drawn by two lions, or as part lion herself. This nurturing goddess is even said to have nursed and cared for lion cubs. Lions in many cultures symbolize courage, loyalty, and leadership, and in a lion pride, the females do the hunting and provide for the family. Consequently, myth links Rhea with having the courage to defy her murderous husband and protect her son, Zeus, who would become the top Olympian god. Additionally, she expressed her maternal nature by assisting other mothers.

MANIFESTING HER POWER

When you need a boost of courage, no matter the reason, look to Rhea to assist you. Obtain a lion figurine and carry it with you. Hold it in your hand when you are feeling weak and think of Rhea's courage entering your own body.

Because Rhea is linked with the easy flow of events and cycles, she can assist you when you want to bring harmony to your life. If you're anxious about a family gathering, for instance, ask Rhea to preside over the event and make everything flow smoothly. Spend time beside a stream, river, or ocean to calm your worries; observe how the water flows naturally without concern for things outside itself.

Sometimes you need to use cunning or deception in order to promote the greater good. In such instances, ask Rhea—who used trickery to stop her husband's infanticide—to be your guide. Carry a piece of agate in your pocket or set the stone in a place where you'll see it often to remind yourself of Rhea's clever ploy.

RHIANNON

"The Celts believed that birds were the heralds of the Otherworld, and their song the speech of that realm, which is why we can nearly understand."

—Lyn Webster Wilde, *Celtic Inspirations*

HISTORY AND MYTHOLOGY

According to mythology, the Welsh goddess Rhiannon rode a white horse and magical birds accompanied her everywhere she went. Rhiannon hailed from the Otherworld, home of the deities and high-ranking spirits in Celtic cosmology. One day, Pwyll Penn Annwfn, king of Dyfed, saw her riding her horse and gave chase but couldn't catch the beauty who was swifter than the wind. He professed his love and begged her to stop. Pwyll followed her into the Otherworld, and there they arranged to marry. Although one of Rhiannon's former suitors delayed the ceremony for a year, eventually she and Pwyll married, and after three years, had a son together.

Unfortunately, the baby mysteriously disappeared. Servants accused Rhiannon of killing the child and Pwyll believed them. He sentenced her to sit for seven years outside the court of Arberth, confessing her crime, and to carry on her back—like a horse—anyone who sought access to the court. The vanished boy, however, turned up in a stable a few years later, became a horseman himself, and was eventually returned to his mother. Rhiannon's unfair punishment ended, and she was restored to her rightful, royal position.

VIRTUES

Rhiannon's reaction to the wrongful accusation for the murder of her son shows her patience, endurance, humility, and willingness to forgive her husband for his cruelty. She also demonstrates forbearance during the

year-long attempt to block her marriage by a jealous suitor and her frustrating three-year wait to bear a child.

Mythology connects the lovely Rhiannon with horses, which symbolize freedom, passion, speed, beauty, and power. Not only does King Pwyll spot her riding a horse that's so fast he can't catch her but the goddess's son turns out to be a horse whisperer as well. She also befriends birds, whose melodic voices inspire healing in mortals and can bring the dead back to life. Rhiannon's association with these magical creatures, as well as her ability to move back and forth between the Otherworld and earth, suggest her shamanic and magical powers.

In addition to being a healer, Rhiannon also inspires poets, singers, and artists of all kinds.

MANIFESTING HER POWER

If you find it necessary to endure in the face of adversity or to tolerate an injustice, ask Rhiannon to give you the resiliency and courage to do so. She'll help you carry the burdens—like a good horse—and keep putting one foot in front of the other, until your physical or emotional trial ends. When you hit a rough patch, remember how Rhiannon bore injustice with grace. You will soon be vindicated. Connect with the goddess by displaying a painting or statue of a horse in your home. You may wish to spend time caring for horses or donate money to animal protection organizations to curry her favor.

Rhiannon can show you how to bring comfort to yourself or someone else through the power of music and sound healing. Play music to ease tension in your own life. Classical music can be especially calming. Take a walk in nature and listen to birdsong. Do you sense the birds trying to communicate and offer healing messages to you?

SARASWATI

"Saraswati the goddess of knowledge, who is praised by the wise, who is the wife of the creator, may she reside on the tip of my tongue."

—www.lotussculpture.com

HISTORY AND MYTHOLOGY

One of the trio of Hindu creator goddesses (along with Lakshmi and Parvati), Saraswati presides over art, music, poetry, language, and knowledge. Some sources say she birthed the Vedas (spiritual texts originating in the ancient Indian subcontinent). Mythology also links her with rivers and the cleansing, healing power of water. Some sources say her domain is the river of consciousness and not necessarily a physical river.

The ancient Hindu epic *Mahabharata* describes her as the heavenly music that inspired her husband, Brahma, as he created the universe. As the story goes, she told the great god that the way to bring order out of chaos was through knowledge. Then she taught him how to think and communicate clearly, and how to connect with the creative power of music, sound, and mantras. Together they formed the universe.

Saraswati transcended the world of the senses, leaving behind all that's base, material, or tied to sensual pleasure and the physical body. Her realm is that of pure mind and enlightened spirit. She's the personification of the light of truth that dissolves chaos, desire, and ignorance.

On the fifth day of spring, some Hindus mark her holiday, known as Vasant Panchami, by teaching children to write the alphabet. Saraswati is worshipped in India, Nepal, Burma, Japan, Cambodia, and other parts of Asia.

VIRTUES

Artists often depict Saraswati as a beautiful woman dressed in a white sari and seated on a white lotus, signifying truth and purity. Sometimes she has two arms, but more often four. In her hands she holds objects that represent her areas of governance: a book, a musical instrument (usually a type of lute), a vessel of water, and a mala (a string of prayer beads, similar to a rosary). Images frequently show her beside a river with her companion, a swan, to symbolize her purity and spiritual wisdom. She's also accompanied by a peacock, whose colorful plumage suggests the arts.

This beautiful goddess is said to speak eloquently with a lyrical voice. She moves with grace, and her countenance conveys serenity. Her divine wisdom inspires writers, artists, and musicians. She's a sort of high-echelon muse.

Saraswati possesses healing ability too. Her connection with water suggests that healing comes through cleansing oneself of physical impurities as well as strife, desire, and the lower energies of human existence. The goddess also draws upon the balancing qualities of sound to produce healing. Water signifies fruitfulness and abundance, for without it, nothing on earth can grow and flourish. Therefore, this creative deity offers earthlings nourishment, prosperity, and well-being.

MANIFESTING HER POWER

Do you seek to expand your knowledge? Are you eager to learn how to think and communicate your ideas more clearly? If so, ask Saraswati to be your teacher. Acquire a mala and offer prayers to the goddess to solicit her aid. She'll lead you to the sources that can further your search for truth and wisdom. However, she may require you to use her knowledge for the good of all, rather than solely for your own gain.

Writers, musicians, and artists of all kinds can gain inspiration from Saraswati. Under her tutelage, you can tap into an elevated realm of creativity and bring forth works that transcend the ordinary. Chant a mantra to her or play a singing bowl, then take up your pen, paintbrush, or musical instrument and relax. Let the goddess guide you into her serene, mystical realm.

SEDNA

"It's said that as long as the Inuit people pay respect to Sedna and honor her with festivals and offerings, she will continue to provide for them."

—Skye Alexander, *Mermaids: The Myths, Legends, and Lore*

HISTORY AND MYTHOLOGY

Also known as Arnakuagsak, Sedna was the most powerful of the Inuit goddesses. Legend says this goddess of the sea started out as a beautiful Inuit woman who had many male admirers, though she rejected every single one. Finally, a trickster seagull beguiled her with promises of a wonderful life if she married him, so she agreed and accompanied him to his island home.

The reality turned out to be far from what she'd expected, and Sedna sent word of her dissatisfaction to her father, who rowed his kayak to the island to bring her home. On the way back, however, a fierce storm (brought on by a flock of seabirds) threatened to capsize their small boat. Sedna's frightened father tossed her overboard, and when she tried to climb back into the boat, he chopped off her fingers.

As she sunk into the sea, down to the land of Adlivun, Sedna transformed into a sea goddess. She retained her woman's head, but sprouted a fishy, mermaid-like tail. Her severed fingers became the sea creatures that provided food for the Inuit people. According to some sources, if the people stop paying homage to her, she whips up storms and restricts access to fish, seals, polar bears, and other sources of food until humans come to their senses and show her proper respect again.

Arctic whalers may have brought the legend and image of Sedna with them in their journeys, carved as figureheads on their ships.

VIRTUES

Sedna's sacrifice produced the sea creatures that made up the diet of the Inuit people who revered her. Sometimes called Mistress of the Sea or Lady of Life and Death, she's seen as a nurturing goddess (with aspects of fertility and protection). She's also a deity of transformation, because through her death, she made it possible for others to survive.

Sedna's story describes the interplay of life and death on our planet. All creatures, in order to survive, must eat something. Something must die so that something else can live. Therefore, Sedna symbolizes the ongoing cycle of life and death, and the power of rejuvenation that results from the sacrifice of one being for the benefit of another. We see parallels to this in many myths, including the Christian story of Jesus' death.

MANIFESTING HER POWER

Sedna shows us how to embrace transformation, how to cope with the tragedies and crises in our lives, and how to emerge courageously from our suffering into more evolved and compassionate beings. Despite being treated cruelly by her father, she created nourishment for the Inuit people. We can learn from her agility and grace. Consider supporting environmental and wildlife organizations that protect sea creatures and their habitats. As you eat, give thanks for the beings that sacrificed their lives so that you may survive.

If you're going through the "dark night of the soul," call upon Sedna to help you bear up under the pain and to extract wisdom from your experience. Acquire an image of a sea creature—a fish, seal, or whale, for example—and display it in a place of honor to reinforce your determination to transcend your current difficulties. Consider swimming with dolphins or going on a whale watch to admire these amazing creatures and connect with the goddess whose suffering created them. You may enjoy visiting an aquarium or watching programs about the ocean's mysteries.

SEKHMET

"More than 1,500 basalt statues of Sekhmet have been uncovered from around Mut's sacred lake. But the main power of Sekhmet lies in a tiny, remote chapel tucked away within the confines of Karnak Temple. The sanctuary of Sekhmet is, for me, one of the most powerful places on the planet."

—Judy Hall, *Crystals and Sacred Sites*

HISTORY AND MYTHOLOGY

Mythology depicts the Egyptian warrior goddess Sekhmet as a fierce lioness who protected the pharaohs in battles. Her name comes from the word *sekem* meaning "power" and she was known as the Powerful One. Daughter of the sun god Ra, this solar deity's scorching breath is said to have formed the deserts, and she's sometimes shown with a disc representing the sun on her head. She married Ptah, god of wisdom (who apparently had a thing for felines, because he was also the husband of the cat goddess Bast).

According to legend, Sekhmet's priestesses engaged in a ritual honoring her in the presence of a different statue of the goddess each day. Supposedly, the rituals were meant to appease the ferocious deity, who's sometimes pictured wearing a blood-red gown. One myth says Ra grew weary of human beings and ordered his lion-daughter to destroy them all. Her bloodlust ended only when she mistook a lake of wine (or perhaps beer dyed with pomegranate juice) for blood, drank it, and became too inebriated to continue on her path of destruction.

At the beginning of the year, ancient Egyptians celebrated Sekhmet's festival with music (to soothe the savage beast) and plenty of wine. The festival coincided with the season when the Nile overflowed its banks and ran red due to mineral deposits. It's possible this flooding inspired the legend of Sekhmet's bloody rampage.

VIRTUES

Mythology tells us that in addition to being a warrior, Sekhmet also possessed great healing power. Her priests and priestesses served as physicians and midwives. She could unleash a plague on those who wronged her or cure the sick with life-saving medicines she devised. In the Egyptian *Book of the Dead*, she's portrayed as both a creator and a destroyer goddess.

Sekhmet is well known for her fiery nature, courage, and willingness to take and protect what's hers. A frightening deity dubbed Lady of Terror, this fearless hunter displays cunning, stealth, and ruthlessness. However, she also embodies dignity and grace. Often she's depicted holding an ankh, symbol of life, and sometimes wearing a headdress around which a deadly cobra coils. A scepter of papyrus signifies her power in Lower Egypt.

One of her closest relationships in the Egyptian pantheon is with Ma'at, goddess of justice and balance, whom Sekhmet protects. Thus, it seems her wrath is not random or unwarranted; indeed, it may be necessary in order to maintain balance between heaven and earth.

MANIFESTING HER POWER

When you feel weak, frightened, or vulnerable, call upon Sekhmet to give you the confidence to face your fears. Dress in red, the color of the heart and assertiveness, to remind yourself of the goddess's courage and your own. Sekhmet urges you to be brave and follow your heart. Understand that you are in control of your choices. Just as Sekhmet could cure or cause illness, you, too, have the power to bring good into your life or to allow destructive energies to take over. Only you can make that determination. At night, drink a glass of red wine (or pomegranate juice) in her honor and think about how to pursue your path in life.

Sekhmet can also show you how to wield power with dignity. Create a collage with pictures that represent leadership to you—and be sure to include a lion in your design. While you work, ask Sekhmet to teach you stealth, cunning, and leadership skills.

SELENE

*"Full Moon Mania is a time for Manifesting dreams....Now is
the perfect time for shouting out loud what you've only dared whisper."*

—Nancy Blair, *Goddesses for Every Season*

HISTORY AND MYTHOLOGY

Better known by her Roman name Luna, Selene is the Greek goddess
of the moon, and she was responsible for guiding the orb in its passage
through the sky each night. Mythology lists her as the daughter of Hyperion and Thea, and sister to Helios (the sun god) and Eos (goddess of
dawn). That also makes her granddaughter to the earth goddess Gaia
and the sky god Ouranos. Every night, this lovely goddess arced through
the dark sky in her silvery chariot, only to relinquish the heavens each
morning to her brother Helios.

According to a popular myth about the goddess, Selene fell in love
with a handsome mortal named Endymion, with whom, some sources
say, she had fifty children who may have represented the weeks of the
year. The goddess didn't want him to grow old and die like other men, so
she asked Zeus to let Endymion sleep forever while she lay in his arms as
his dream lover. Other legends tell us Endymion loved Hera, wife of Zeus,
and because he couldn't have her, he asked Zeus to put him into a state
of eternal sleep, presumably so he could avoid dealing with the problem.
Both stories point to our desire to enjoy love in a divine (some might say
fantasy) world, and to transcend the mundane in order to connect with
the mystical.

VIRTUES

Artists often depict Selene riding in a chariot drawn by a pair of winged
white horses during her nightly journey across the sky. Like other moon

deities of the ancient world—Artemis, Hathor, Hera—she sometimes wears a headdress fashioned like a cow's curving horns, whose shape represents the crescent moon. The horns hold a lunar disc to show her connection with the moon and feminine cycles of fertility.

We link the moon and Selene with the emotions, intuition, and imagination. Romance is her specialty. She's a favorite of poets and inspires love poems in particular. Some sources credit Selene as a teacher of magic, and magic workers often time spells according to the moon's phases. Certainly, the night is a time of magic and mystery. Wiccans feel a strong connection to the moon and hold rituals during the new and full moons.

MANIFESTING HER POWER

Ask Selene to enhance your creativity and intuition—she can inspire your imagination and help you pen beautiful poetry or create other artwork. Track her movements through the sky and your reactions to them. On the full moon, when she shines brightest, make an offering of something silver to her.

Want more romance in your life? Call upon Selene to open your heart and sweeten your love. Eat by moonlight and dance under the starry sky. At night, sit outside with a lover and watch the moon rise into the heavens. Write a poem to thank the goddess for her assistance.

Plan magic spells to harmonize with the moon's cycles and invite Selene to lend a hand. If your intention is to attract or increase something, do a spell when the moon is waxing. If you want to release or decrease something, cast your spell during the moon's waning stage.

SHAKTI

"Every mother and every beloved is forced to become the carrier and embodiment of this omnipresent and ageless image, which corresponds to the deepest reality in man."

—C.G. Jung, *Collected Works*, "The Syzygy: Anima and Animus"

HISTORY AND MYTHOLOGY

In Hindu mythology Shakti is said to be the primal, unknowable, and dynamic feminine force in the universe. Rather than existing as a distinct personage herself, her divine essence and energy are expressed through many goddesses, as aspects of the Great Goddess or Devi. We see her in Durga, in Lakshmi, in Parvati, in Saraswati, and in Kali. Through them she reveals many faces and performs many roles. By extension, she also shows herself in all mortal women.

Usually seen as a creator goddess, Shakti is the consort and complement of Shiva, the god of destruction. She's also a mother goddess, for her feminine power is necessary for life to exist. According to texts known as the Tantras, Shakti, the feminine force, contains within it the masculine principle; thus, she is the original, supreme, and eternal deity. As the ultimate creative power, she didn't need Shiva—he needed her. It's also said that no god could accomplish anything without her, and that each god had a goddess—an expression of Shakti—who was his soul.

VIRTUES

Hindu mythology tells us Shakti is the source of all, the creator of all, and the soul of all. In Sanskrit, her name derives from the word *shak*, meaning "to be able" or "empowerment." Her essence gives vitality, substance, and power to all beings. She's also the embodiment of beauty and well-being:

180

the life force that animates matter and supports eternal youth. Always flowing, flexible, both active and receptive, she's a divine agent of positive change—without her, stagnation and death result.

Shakti's loving energy offers her devotees protection against harmful beings and relief from suffering. Legend says she has knowledge in the magical arts and uses her skills to banish evil.

Myth also connects the goddess with intelligence, inspiration, and communication. Sometimes referred to as Divine Mind, Shakti elevates human thinking, speech, and spiritual development. Her energy is said to reside in the root chakra at the base of the spine, and it can be raised through meditation, yogic practices, and chanting mantras.

MANIFESTING HER POWER

Because Shakti is the source of all, you are always connected to her—she abides within you and you within her. She can aid you in any area of your life, in any endeavor you undertake. Consider setting up an altar to Shakti. Lay a beautiful Indian shawl on top of it. Adorn the altar with flowers and colorful images of Hindu goddesses. As her name suggests, Shakti empowers you to create whatever you seek. She can inspire creative projects of all sorts—artwork, literary compositions, and imaginative and useful inventions.

Some sources say that to honor Shakti, you must honor all women and recognize the goddess within each one of them. To attract her favor, perform acts of kindness and generosity toward women in your life, and women in need all over the world. Dedicate yourself to causes that improve conditions for women everywhere.

SITA

"Loyalty and devotion lead to bravery. Bravery leads to the spirit of self-sacrifice. The spirit of self-sacrifice creates trust in the power of love."
—Morihei Ueshiba, founder of the martial art aikido

HISTORY AND MYTHOLOGY

According to Hindu mythology, Sita was the first wife of the god Rama. Her name means "furrow," because of her unusual birth: she emerged from a furrow in the ground made by King Janaka as he plowed his field, which suggests the goddess incarnated on earth. As the adopted daughter of Janaka, she's sometimes called Janaki.

The ancient epic *Ramayana* tells us that a family disagreement led to Rama being exiled for fourteen years. Sita went with him. While the couple traveled about, a horrible demon with ten heads and twenty arms kidnapped Sita and carried her off to his kingdom. Because she was devoted to her husband, the beautiful Sita remained pure during her imprisonment, and eventually Rama managed to rescue her after winning a number of battles. Sita even endured a trial by fire to prove her chastity. The couple then reclaimed their rightful throne and lived happily ever after.

Another story says Rama was still suspicious of his wife and sent her away to the forest where Sita gave birth to twin sons. The god finally claimed them as his own. Sita, still angry at Rama for his mistreatment of her, called on Mother Earth (from which she'd been born) to release her from the unhappiness of her existence. The earth swallowed Sita, and Rama drowned himself so he could follow her into the next world.

VIRTUES

Sita is revered for her goodness, honesty, and her devotion to her husband. She sacrifices her comfortable home and goes with him when

Rama's family banishes him. During her time in captivity by a demon, she firmly resists the advances of her captor and remains true to her husband. She walks through fire to prove her faithfulness. She endures the unfair exile Rama imposes on her and bears him two sons.

Not only is the goddess loyal but she's also brave and strong in the face of adversity. Sita never sacrifices her principles. She maintains her honor and, in the end, she's vindicated. Thus, her story depicts the difficulties women endure and the virtues traditionally considered desirable in an Indian wife.

Her birth from a field makes her a goddess of agriculture and a personification of Mother Earth. In this role, Sita is linked with fertility and abundance. Her birth, life, and death also represent the concept of reincarnation.

MANIFESTING HER POWER

The goddess Sita brings hope and courage during times of struggle. If you're in a difficult relationship but don't want to leave it, ask Sita to lend you her strength. She'll offer guidance that can sustain you as you work through problems. To align yourself with Sita's power, seek a deeper connection with the earth. Plant flowers, herbs, or vegetables and care for them with love and patience.

Look at the relationships in your own life. Do you feel you are loyal to your friends and family members? Remember Sita's devotion to her husband, and use her example to strengthen your own relationships. This may be as easy as sending a long-lost friend a text or calling to touch base.

During trials and tribulations, Sita encourages you to remain true to yourself and never falter from your core beliefs. Let her show you how to hold your head high when other people question you or treat you unfairly. Through adversity, we grow stronger. The goddess teaches that the purpose of life on earth, with all its challenges, is the growth of the soul. Walk in the woods and observe the old trees. Think how much they've endured through the years. Touch their bark and ask them—and Sita— to share their wisdom with you.

SOPHIA

"You of the whirling wings, / circling, encompassing energy of God: / you quicken the world in your clasp. / One wing soars in heaven, / one wing sweeps the earth, / and the third flies all around us. / Praise to Sophia! / Let all the earth praise her!"

—Hildegard von Bingen, eleventh-century abbess and mystic

HISTORY AND MYTHOLOGY

In Gnostic tradition Sophia is considered the goddess of wisdom (her name means "wisdom" in Greek). She appears in Anthroposophy and Theosophy too, and is honored by Wiccans and Neo-Pagans. Some Judeo-Christian sources speak of her as the wisdom of God or as God's female soul, an aspect of divinity rather than a distinct goddess. The Christian mystic Thomas Merton called her God's "glory." Biblical stories sometimes name her as King Solomon's wife. She was especially significant within the Eastern Orthodox Church. Hagia Sophia (Church of the Holy Wisdom), in Istanbul, is named for this aspect of Christian mysticism.

In addition to her role as goddess of wisdom, myths describe Sophia as a creator goddess who birthed both the feminine and masculine forces of the universe, thus bringing the material world into being. She's said to have deeply loved humankind and wanted to share the gift of knowledge with them—wise leaders, including King Solomon, relied on her guidance.

VIRTUES

Sophia's sacred bird is the dove, also seen as a symbol of peace. Some sources say Sophia was the angel/deity who, in the form of a dove, came to tell the Virgin Mary she would give birth to Jesus.

A loving and compassionate deity, Sophia embodies truth. Through communicating wisdom to the world, she encourages hope and eases the suffering that results from despair. She teaches us to open our minds and hearts and learn the great truths that would set humankind free. She's also a protector goddess whose guidance, if heeded, can prevent mistakes, strife, and misery. During times of stress, she gives strength and shows the way to resolve conflict. The understanding that Sophia offers can chase away darkness and confusion, replacing it with justice and peace on earth.

MANIFESTING HER POWER

When confusion, misunderstanding, or chaos threaten your peace of mind, call upon Sophia to enhance your vision so you can see the big picture. On a clear day, go to the top of a hill or another high place where you can look out into the distance. Seek to "know" not only with your intellect, but also with your intuition (often linked with the feminine principle). Ask the goddess to give you the wisdom to understand a murky situation and see things clearly. Sophia can disperse the dark clouds of distress and let clarity shine through.

Sophia can help you feel compassion for your fellow humans, even those you dislike (*especially* those you dislike). When you find yourself getting angry with someone who pushes your buttons or you're tempted to judge others for wrongdoing, ask this gentle goddess to share with you the love she feels for all beings that myth says she brought into the world. Contemplate an image of a dove, a symbol of peace. Even just imagining how this bird can fly away when necessary, letting the wind carry it wherever it needs to go, can help you distance yourself from the anger you feel. If possible, observe doves in nature and listen to their lilting song as you feel unhappiness melting away.

SPIDER WOMAN

"Spider Woman made all the plants, the flowers, the bushes, and the trees. Likewise she made the birds and animals, again using earth and singing the Creation Song. When all this was done, she made human beings, using yellow, red, white, and black earth mixed with her saliva."
—from the stories of Oswald White Bear Fredericks and his wife Naomi, www.gly.uga.edu/railsback/CS/CSFourCreations.html

HISTORY AND MYTHOLOGY

According to some versions of the creation myths of the Hopi and other tribes in the southwestern United States, Spider Woman (or Spider Grandmother) wove the world into being. Her great web connected the sun, moon, earth, and stars. In one legend this creator goddess fashioned a tubular channel between heaven and earth (like a cosmic birth canal), culminating at the Grand Canyon. Souls then descended through this tube to incarnate on earth. In another tale, the goddess wrapped entities who were destined to incarnate in hollow reeds and floated them on the seas to earth. A Navajo myth says she rescued beings who'd caused trouble on their way toward earthly incarnation by flinging a net to them so they wouldn't drown.

Still another story says she encourages sweet dreams and positive communication between the divine realm and humans. She accomplishes this via web-like "dreamcatchers" that people still hang above their beds to capture insights and messages from the ancestors. Other tales say Spider Woman brought fire to humankind and ferried worthy souls into the higher realms after their bodies died.

VIRTUES

Spider Woman links each of us to everything in the universe—the seen and the unseen, the physical and the supernatural. Her web is the energetic matrix that spins out into eternity, containing all knowledge and experience. We affect and are affected by everything else. Just as a spider senses even the slightest touch to a thread in her web, the goddess alerts us to the many influences that impact us both positively and negatively.

This goddess sits at the center of the universe and holds it all together. She joins all beings on earth and elsewhere via her intricate web. She doesn't just birth the cosmos and those who inhabit it, she delicately manages its ebb and flow. In so doing, she promotes unity, harmony, and mutually beneficial interaction among all her creations.

Spider Woman is often revered as a helper deity, a teacher and guide. Legend says she taught human beings to weave, which has both practical and spiritual implications. Under her tutelage, people learned to appreciate beauty and to create it themselves.

MANIFESTING HER POWER

Ask Spider Woman to help you understand your dreams. What are they telling you? How can you apply your nighttime explorations in your waking life? Hang a dreamcatcher above your bed to capture dream experiences and filter out nightmares. Let Spider Woman bless you with restful sleep. Also consider keeping a dream journal so you can track the insights you receive while you're asleep and review them when you're awake.

Do you feel disconnected from other people, perhaps even those in your own community or family? Do you wonder about your origins, not only the physical ones but the spiritual source from which you evolved? If so, ask Spider Woman to help you relink to your ancestors, spirit guides, guardian angels, etc. Ask her to show you how you are aligned with all things, on earth and in the higher realms. Seek beauty in its many forms, perhaps by attending exhibits of crafts such as weaving, quiltmaking, etc. If you can weave or knit, make this a meditation to her.

If you come across a spider's web, take a moment to observe its intricacies and complex design. Give thanks to Spider Woman for her creation.

TARA

"I cannot help but believe that Tara was standing by whispering in scientists' ears as they launched Pioneer 10 into space…in 1972, bearing a message of peace to anyone who might find it."

—Patricia Telesco, *365 Goddess: A Daily Guide to the Magic and Inspiration of the Goddess*

HISTORY AND MYTHOLOGY

Hindu goddess of peace, cooperation, and unity, the beautiful Tara offers us insight into the workings of the universe and our place in it. Her name means "star" in Sanskrit, and like the star, she brings hope. She's also revered in Buddhism, which tells us she floated on a lotus blossom in a lake of the bodhisattva Avalokitesvara's tears. Legend describes her as his companion and counterpart.

Tara takes many forms (some sources say twenty-one) and in each she expresses a different facet of her divinity. As White Tara, she embodies compassion and is known as the mother of all buddhas. Pictured as a beautiful young woman, she has pure white skin (indicating her purity) and seven eyes—in addition to the usual two, she has one in the center of her forehead, one on each palm, and one on the sole of each foot. As Green Tara, she serves humankind as a protector and guide. Often she's depicted as a graceful young woman with green skin, and some sources link her with Mother Earth. As Yellow Tara, she brings abundance. Like the Hindu goddess Lakshmi, she's connected with water and the river Ganges. In her black and blue depictions, she resembles the fierce destroyer goddess Kali.

VIRTUES

Tara expresses herself in many ways (symbolized by colors), and each depiction relates to a special role and responsibility, including mother, protector, savior, sage, healer, warrior, and guardian of heaven, earth, and the underworld.

Among these many manifestations, she's best known as White Tara and Green Tara. In these forms she displays compassion, forgiveness, unconditional love, selflessness, devotion, protection, healing, and purity. Her great wisdom is that of the buddhas, and she shares with humankind the knowledge of oneness, that all life is entwined and interdependent. As a mother goddess, Tara nurtures all life. She watches over human beings and guides them through their earthly endeavors, giving them strength and courage as they tread the path to enlightenment.

MANIFESTING HER POWER

Call upon Green Tara, the protector face of the goddess, to give you strength and protection during difficult times. Ask her to be your guide and guardian as you journey through life. She'll show you how to overcome obstacles and endure hardships—not only of a physical nature, but also those you encounter on the spiritual path.

White Tara can help you find compassion and forgiveness. If you believe someone has wronged you, ask the goddess to give you the inner strength necessary to release anger and conflict within yourself. She also teaches that we are all one, and that what we do to others, we do to ourselves. Awareness of this truth opens your heart and mind to peace.

To attune yourself with Tara's energies, dress in clothing of the color that represents the attributes and powers you seek: white for compassion, green for protection, yellow for prosperity, and so on. You can also acquire candles in each color and burn them when you need extra support from this goddess.

TEFNUT

*"In Egypt, they worship lions, and there is a city
named after them….The lions have temples and numerous
spaces in which to roam."*

—Aelian, ancient Roman historian

HISTORY AND MYTHOLOGY

This Egyptian goddess's name translates as *tef*—"moist"—and
nu—"sky." Thus, she was seen as the deity who brought life-giving rain
(as well as mist and dew) from the sky to an arid country that could not
have flourished without her aid. Ironically, however, she was also considered a sun goddess and known as the Eye of Ra.

Myths tell us Tefnut was the daughter of the creator god Ra (a.k.a.,
Amun or Atum). She's also the mother of the sky goddess Nut and the
earth god Geb, making her an honored matriarch in the Egyptian pantheon, and the grandmother of some of its most important deities: Isis,
Osiris, Nephthys, Horus, and Set. She married Shu (who was also her
twin brother), the god of air and light.

One myth about her (which may describe an actual meteorological
event) says Tefnut became angry with her father and abandoned Egypt
for Nubia, taking all the land's moisture with her. As drought descended
on the country, Tefnut's husband and the scribe-god Thoth went after
her. They gave her a calming red drink (which may have been wine) and
convinced her to come home. When she returned, her father shed happy
tears that created the first human beings.

VIRTUES

Mythology links Tefnut with the lioness, and early artists sometimes
rendered her as a woman with a lion's head, suggesting her regal

countenance and authority. Along with other leonine deities, such as Sekhmet, she was worshipped at the city of Leontopolis. She's also depicted wearing a solar disc (indicating her link to Ra) surrounded by cobras on her head. Often she's shown holding an ankh, a symbol of eternal life, and a scepter, a symbol of power and leadership.

A painting of Tefnut in the tomb of the pharaoh Ramses II suggests ancient Egyptians also connected the goddess with life after death. One story says this deity of water provided libations to the deceased as they made their way into the afterlife. As goddess of moisture, she's seen as a nurturing and fertile deity, for life could not exist without her.

MANIFESTING HER POWER

Call upon this goddess of rain to assist you by "watering" a project or venture you've undertaken. She can provide nourishment to help your ideas blossom and flourish. Consider planting flowers or herbs in her name to thank Tefnut. Water them as you focus on the growth and success of your goal.

Take a few minutes to listen to the rain the next time it storms, or listen to rain recordings to calm your nerves. Think of how rain can wash away dirt and apply this cleansing to your own life. You may even consider purchasing a rain stick to mimic the sound of rain when you need to wash away broken expectations or pain.

We associate lions with royalty, courage, and strength. Therefore, this leonine goddess can help you take charge of a situation and demonstrate your leadership ability. If you feel inadequate, weak, or anxious, ask Tefnut to lend you her power. When the moon is in the zodiac sign Leo, acquire a figurine or picture of a lion (or of the lion-headed goddess) and display it in a place of honor, where you'll see it often and remember that Tefnut is by your side.

TIAMAT

*"Babylonian myth said that before the world was
created, there was only Tiamat, dragon of the bitter waters
and the sweet springs. In the deepest dark,
before all being arose, She gave birth to light."*

—Nancy Blair, *Goddesses for Every Season*

HISTORY AND MYTHOLOGY

Babylonian mythology tells us Tiamat was the mother of everything, including all the other gods and goddesses. This powerful creator deity was the personification of the ocean, from which life evolved. Usually she's depicted as a female water dragon. Some stories say she split her body in two, thereby forming heaven and earth from the watery void and bringing order out of chaos.

According to some legends, she had a consort named Apsu, god of fresh water. Together, by mingling salt water and fresh, they brought into being Lachmu and Lachamu, who became the parents of Ansar and Kisar, and the grandparents of Anu and Ea. But after a while, Tiamat grew annoyed with her descendants, so she and Apsu decided to eat them. When Ea discovered the plan, he killed Apsu. The angry Tiamat, in retaliation, birthed a slew of monsters and set them against her relatives, under the direction of her new mate Kingu.

However, Ea's son, the god Marduk, managed to kill Tiamat. Water gushed from her eyes, forming the Tigris and the Euphrates Rivers. In some versions of the myth, Marduk cut her body up into a lot of little pieces and used them to form everything in the universe. From Kingu's blood he fashioned the first humans.

VIRTUES

This primordial mother goddess was the source of all that exists, on earth and elsewhere in the universe. Her power was enormous. The Genesis story of creation calls to mind Tiamat's myth when it says, "and the earth was without form, and void; and darkness was upon the face of the deep. And the Spirit of God moved upon the face of the waters."

Shown as a water dragon, she's also fierce and dangerous, even bloodthirsty, for she kills her own kin (which may symbolize an actual physical event, such as a flood, or the ocean's ability to provide as well as destroy). In this sense, Tiamat is both a creator and a destroyer deity. She decides who lives and who dies. Eventually, the goddess is slain by a god, which may represent the rise of patriarchal cultures and the demise of matriarchal ones. However, even in death she continues to create the sun, moon, planets, and stars.

MANIFESTING HER POWER

Call upon Tiamat to help you accomplish any project, no matter how large. This dragon deity combines the creative energies of fire and water, so she's ideally suited to ignite your imagination. Acquire three floating candles in a color that appeals to you. Fill a large flame-resistant pot, cauldron, or bathtub with water, then light the candles and set them to float on the water. As you gaze at the flames, sense Tiamat's inspiration flowing through you.

Do you need to get rid of something so that you can continue growing and creating the life you truly desire? Because Tiamat is both a creator and a destroyer, she can assist you in the process. Acquire some Dragon's Blood ink and, on a sheet of paper, write what you wish to eliminate as well as what you want to attract or foster. Make a small fire in a cauldron, fireproof pot, or charcoal grill, and drop the paper into the flames. When it's finished burning, pour cold water on the fire—the steam will carry your intention to Tiamat.

WANGMU NIANGNIANG

"The Queen Mother of the West obtained it [the Dao] and took up her seat at Mount Shaoguang. No one knows her beginning; no one knows her end."
—Elisabeth Benard and Beverly Moon, *Goddesses Who Rule*

HISTORY AND MYTHOLOGY

Worshipped in China and other Asian countries, Wangmu Niangniang is known by many names including Queen Mother of the West. The personification of yin, the primal feminine force in the universe, she's the epitome of female power. Although early depictions represent her as a rather nasty deity who wreaked havoc on humankind by sending them plagues and other hardships, later legends softened her reputation and presented her as a goddess of longevity and prosperity.

Artists sometimes show Wangmu Niangniang in her magnificent palace atop Mount Kunlan in western China (which may be a mythical place rather than the Mount Kunlan of today), accompanied by other lesser goddesses and wearing a headdress with peaches dangling from it. According to myth, her paradise by the Jade Lake was a popular meeting place for deities and boasted an otherworldly garden with rare peach trees that produced fruit only once every 3,000 years. Anyone who ate the goddess's peaches at her legendary banquets became immortal.

Sometimes she's portrayed as the wife of the Jade Emperor (ruler of heaven), with whom she had seven daughters. Legend says that at the seventh hour of the seventh day of the seventh month the goddess descends to earth to commune with humans and establish harmony on our planet.

Wangmu Niangniang is often connected with Taoism. Some accounts say she met with the noted Chinese philosopher Lao Tzu and inspired him to compose the *Tao Te Ching*, Taoism's sacred text.

VIRTUES

Considered to be the top goddess in Chinese mythology, she oversees all the other female deities and serves as their guardian, teacher, and judge. By extension, she also guides and protects Taoist women. Wangmu Niangniang gives special attention to independent women who don't kowtow to male-dominant conventions. She understands the importance of the Divine Feminine and knows yin is the complement of yang, not subservient to it. An early feminist, she supports equality between the sexes and encourages women and girls to fulfill their gifts and aspirations.

Generally seen as a benevolent deity, Wangmu Niangniang brings mortals health, wealth, and happiness. She nourishes all things with the loving-kindness of a caring mother. The goddess of life and immortality, she's reached a state of perfection and maintains balance in the universe. According to some sources, she also governs the stars.

MANIFESTING HER POWER

Free-spirited women who reject patriarchy can call upon Wangmu Niangniang to support their objectives and strengthen their pride in being female. If you feel you've been unfairly treated due to your gender or you're championing equality in your professional or personal life, ask the goddess for her support. Read passages from the *Tao Te Ching* and/or reflect upon scenes depicted in Taoist artwork to gain insight into the balance between yin and yang. Collect some of your favorite feminist quotes and display them prominently for inspiration. You may even want to pick up a collection of feminist poetry to read when you need a boost of motivation.

Do you seek a long, healthy, wealthy, comfortable life? If so, Wangmu Niangniang can show you the way to achieve your goals. As you invite her wise counsel, eat a peach and allow her guidance to come through to you. Be sure to announce that you are eating the fruit in her honor. Remember to offer the goddess some of the delicious fruit too.

WHITE BUFFALO CALF WOMAN

"The arrival of the white buffalo is like the second coming of Christ….It will bring about purity of mind, body, and spirit and unify all nations—black, red, yellow, and white."
—Floyd Hand Looks For Buffalo, Oglala Medicine Man

HISTORY AND MYTHOLOGY

Some indigenous people of the North American plains say that White Buffalo Calf Woman taught human beings how to live peacefully and be good stewards of the earth. According to one version of her myth, two young hunters encountered the goddess dressed in white buckskin. One man started to force himself on her, but the deity, who could intuit his motives, dissolved him into a pile of bones. She told the other man to return to his tribe and prepare for her visit.

Four days later, the goddess, in the form of a white buffalo calf, floated to earth on a cloud. The calf rolled on the ground, changing colors from white to black to yellow to red—the four colors of the medicine wheel. She then transformed herself into a beautiful young woman holding a bundle that contained sacred objects, including the pipe.

White Buffalo Calf Woman schooled the people in dancing, singing, rites, prayer, and ceremony. Then she departed, leaving the bundle in their keeping. However, she promised to return—again as a white buffalo calf—when the world fell into chaos and she would restore harmony. Perhaps she is already here, for in 1994 on a farm in Wisconsin a rare white buffalo calf was born. Since then, two more white buffalo calves have been born on the same farm, the most recent in 2006.

VIRTUES

White Buffalo Calf Woman understands the interconnectedness of all things in the universe. Through her wisdom and leadership, she guided the people of the plains, teaching them the secrets of the earth and how to walk in balance with all life. The four colors she took on while in the body of a calf also represent the four races, signifying the oneness of all peoples.

The goddess is credited with bringing sacred traditions and arts to humankind. A visionary, White Buffalo Calf Woman conveys messages from the divine realm to the mundane one. With her power of prophecy, she can see a coming time of chaos; however, she also offers hope with her promise to return. The white buffalo calf, a most sacred symbol among many tribes, represents rebirth.

Legend says that after the deity's visit, the buffalo herds increased and abundance returned to the land. Thus, she's connected with prosperity and fruitfulness. Although White Buffalo Calf Woman is known as a goddess of peace and compassion, she won't tolerate harmful behavior, as is shown by the way she annihilated the mythical young hunter. When she returns, she may destroy the wicked and restore peace.

MANIFESTING HER POWER

White Buffalo Calf Woman can reveal to you the sacredness of All That Is and teach you the mysteries of existence. Draw and color an image of the medicine wheel and reflect on its meaning. Ask the goddess to show you how to stop struggling and coexist harmoniously with others on the planet. Her loving guidance can keep you on the right road, leaving behind harmful ideas and behaviors, thereby gaining peace and a sense of purpose in your life.

If you've experienced a difficult time and feel discouraged or depleted, ask White Buffalo Calf Woman to give you hope for the future. If you've suffered losses, she can help you see the way to renewed abundance.

Build a small fire and sprinkle tobacco in the flames as an offering to the goddess.

If you feel closed off from others, ask the White Buffalo Calf Woman to assist you in becoming more open and accepting. Study different cultures and beliefs to see how others live. Try eating a different cuisine once a week or once a month, to experience a part of other cultures firsthand. Dedicate each new meal to the White Buffalo Calf Woman and thank her for her patience.

XOCHIQUETZAL

"Learn her, and cherish her, respect her, and love her; for
she is so much more than a pretty face, she is a soul on fire."

—T.B. LaBerge

HISTORY AND MYTHOLOGY

The Aztec goddess of love, beauty, sexuality, art, and crafts, Xochiquetzal
was the wife of the rain god Tlaloc. Her name translates as *xochi* meaning "flower" and *quetzal* meaning "feather," specifically the bluish-green
feathers of a bird known as a quetzal.

Legend says Tezcatlipoca, god of the night, abducted the pretty Xochiquetzal and forced her to be his wife and live with him in what some stories describe as the cold, dark realm of dead deities. However, he eventually
released her. According to some sources, she also had two other husbands
and is the mother of the god Quetzalcoatl. She lived in Tamoanchan, one of
thirteen heavens in Aztec mythology, where she created human beings and
served as a liaison between the deities and earthlings.

On her visits to earth, she heard people's confessions and, if she
chose to, she forgave their sins. Each year at harvest time, Xochiquetzal's
followers visited her temple to seek absolution from the goddess. At the
festival of Atamalqualiztli, held once every eight years, her people celebrated for eight days, during which they adorned her temple with flowers, danced, and ate corn tamales. According to some sources, a young
woman who symbolized the goddess was sacrificed at the festival.

VIRTUES

Xochiquetzal presided over agriculture in Aztec culture and was responsible for the earth's fruitfulness. She loved all plants but especially flowers, and artists often depicted her with birds and flowers.

Images portray her as a beautiful young woman who reveled in luxury, sensual and sexual pleasure, music, and dancing. Unlike some fertility deities, Xochiquetzal encouraged sex for enjoyment as well as for procreation. In her role as goddess of love and fertility, she had the power to cast love spells. She could also absolve people of misdeeds, particularly those of a sexual nature.

As the goddess of arts and crafts, Xochiquetzal inspired artisans to fashion handsome products that served practical purposes, including textiles, metalwork, and pottery.

MANIFESTING HER POWER

The lovely and lusty Xochiquetzal can offer advice to improve your sex life. Ask her to bring you a new lover or teach you how to increase the passion in an existing relationship. You may consider burning incense to invite Xochiquetzal into your intimate moments. You can ask her to share her beauty secrets with you too. Plant flowers in her honor or acquire a pretty plant and tend it with loving care as a way of showing thanks for the goddess's assistance.

Artists and craftspeople can gain inspiration from Xochiquetzal. Study colorful Aztec artwork to get ideas. You may want to acquire a piece of pottery, jewelry, or fabric decorated with Aztec designs or display an image of the goddess in a place where you'll see it often. Even if your own work is vastly different in style, Xochiquetzal can lend you creative energy and boost your artistic output. You can also collect vibrant gemstones to help inspire creativity, such as turquoise, malachite, ruby, yellow topaz, and red tiger's eye. Examine the intricacies of their patterns for inspiration.

Do you feel you've wronged someone? If so, ask Xochiquetzal to pardon you and show you how to make amends. Give corn tamales as an apology gift and as an offering to the goddess. You can also cook a dinner of corn tamales in honor of the goddess. Be sure to thank her for her assistance as you prepare and eat your meal.

YEMAYA

"Yemaya remind[s] us that even the worst catastrophes can be endured
and that, with her help, we can learn to negotiate the ebbs and
flows of change in our lives with her wisdom, courage, and grace."
—Sharon Turnbull, www.goddessgift.com

HISTORY AND MYTHOLOGY

The ocean goddess Yemaya (or Yemoja) abides at the heart of several African religions. Her full name Yey Omo Eja means "mother whose children are the fish." Often she's depicted as a mermaid. Legend tells us Yemaya started out as the goddess of Nigeria's Ogun River. When her African followers were brought across the ocean to the New World, the goddess came with them and watched over them as they endured the arduous voyage and travails of slavery. Along the way, Yemaya's powers expanded, and she gained dominion over the ocean as well. She's also worshipped in parts of South America.

Yemaya is said to be the mother of us all, for human beings evolved from the ocean. She was the wife of Aganju, god of the land (although myths say she had several other husbands too); mother to Oya, goddess of the wind; and sister of the river goddess Oshun (although some sources say Oshun is Yemaya's daughter). According to folklore, the goddess's energy flows through seashells. Reputedly she gave shells to human beings so they could listen to her voice.

VIRTUES

Yemaya represents the uppermost portion of the ocean, not its depths. This is the part that contains most of the sea life, the source of nourishment, and this mother deity generously provides for her human children. Therefore, she's also connected with prosperity.

Like many fertility goddesses, she protects women and children. She cares for mothers and their infants during pregnancy and childbirth and can also cure infertility. As befits a fertility deity, Yemaya exudes a potent sexuality. Artists often portray her as voluptuous, with large breasts, hips, and buttocks that suggest her creative power. The rolling tides symbolize the motion of her undulating walk. She wears seven blue-and-white skirts that signify the seven seas. When she dances—which she loves to do—her skirts ripple and cause waves to appear. Despite her caring, comforting, and compassionate nature, Yemaya can be temperamental—just like the ocean she personifies. Legend says this protective goddess drowns those who harm her children.

We often connect water with intuition, and Yemaya is known for her skill at divination. She uses cowrie shells (which resemble the vulva) to tell fortunes.

MANIFESTING HER POWER

Like most mother-fertility goddesses, Yemaya helps women and children and serves as a cosmic midwife. Ask her to keep you safe through pregnancy and delivery. If you wish to become pregnant, call on her for assistance. Consider wearing a necklace made of cowrie shells to attract her powers of fertility and protection.

Would you like to improve your intuition? Do you want to know what the future holds or to see beyond your ordinary range of vision? Invite Yemaya to open your "sixth sense." Hold a shell to your ear and listen to Yemaya's soft voice speaking to you. You can also collect small shells and make an altar dedicated to Yemaya. You may even choose to place seashells around your window frames to attract Yemaya's protection. When you are feeling anxious, rub the shells between your fingers and feel the grooves of the waves that brought them ashore. Breathe deeply and focus on the rhythm of your breath moving up and down like the ocean tide.

APPENDIX A: GODDESS BY ORIGIN

The following is a list of the goddesses arranged by their cultural origins.

AUSTRALIAN ABORIGINAL
Rainbow Serpent

AFRICAN
Mami Wata
Odudua
Oshun
Oya
Yemaya

AZTEC
Coatlicue
Xochiquetzal

BABYLONIAN
Ishtar
Tiamat

CELTIC
Aine
Badb
Branwen
Brigid
Cerridwen
Danu
Medb
The Morrigan
Rhiannon

CHINESE
Chang'e
Kuan Yin
Wangmu Niangniang

EGYPTIAN
Anuket
Bast
Hathor
Isis
Ma'at
Meskhenet
Nephthys
Nut
Sekhmet
Tefnut

GERMANIC
Ostara

GNOSTIC
Sophia

GREEK (ROMAN)
Aphrodite (Venus)
Artemis (Diana)
Athena (Minerva)
Demeter (Ceres)
Eos (Aurora)
Eris (Discordia)
Gaia (Terra)
Hecate (Trivia)
Hera (Juno)
Hestia (Vesta)
Iris
Nemesis (Invidia)
Nike (Victoria)
Persephone (Proserpina)
Rhea (Ops)
Selene (Luna)

HAWAIIAN
Pele

HEBREW
Lilith

HINDU
Aditi
Durga
Kali
Lakshmi
Parvati
Saraswati
Shakti
Sita
Tara

INCAN
Mama Quilla
Pachamama

INUIT
Sedna

JAPANESE
Amaterasu
Izanami-no-Mikoto

MAYAN
Ix Chel

NATIVE AMERICAN
Changing Woman
Spider Woman
White Buffalo Calf Woman

NORSE
Freya
Frigg
Hel

SUMERIAN
Ereshkigal
Inanna

APPENDIX B: GODDESS BY VIRTUE

The following is a list of the goddesses arranged by their major virtues and symbols.

ART/INSPIRATION

Athena
Bast
Brigid
Oshun
Rainbow Serpent
Saraswati
Shakti
Xochiquetzal

BEAUTY

Amaterasu
Aphrodite
Bast
Hathor
Hera
Inanna
Oshun
Rhiannon
Xochiquetzal

CHAOS

Eris
Oya
Pele

CHILDBIRTH

Aphrodite
Coatlicue
Frigg
Gaia
Hathor
Ix Chel
Meskhenet
Selene
Yemaya

COURAGE/STRENGTH

Artemis
Branwen
Hera
Inanna
Lilith
Nike
Rhea
Rhiannon
Sekhmet
Sita

CREATOR GODDESS
Aditi
Changing Woman
Coatlicue
Danu
Durga
Gaia
Izanami-no-Mikoto
Mama Quilla
Odudua
Pachamama
Pele
Rainbow Serpent
Shakti
Spider Woman
Tiamat

DEATH
Ereshkigal
Hel
Izanami-no-Mikoto
Kali
Ma'at
Meskhenet
The Morrigan
Nephthys
Oya
Persephone

DESTINY
Badb
Freya
Frigg
Ma'at
Meskhenet
The Morrigan
White Buffalo Calf Woman

EARTH GODDESS AND NATURE
Aine
Artemis
Changing Woman
Coatlicue
Demeter
Gaia
Ix Chel
Mami Wata
Odudua
Oshun
Ostara
Rainbow Serpent
Pachamama
White Buffalo Calf Woman
Xochiquetza

FERTILITY AND MOTHERHOOD
Aine
Anuket
Aphrodite
Bast
Branwen
Brigid
Cerridwen
Changing Woman
Coatlicue
Danu
Demeter
Frigg
Gaia
Inanna
Ishtar
Isis
Ix Chel
Izanami-no-Mikoto
Mami Wata
Odudua
Oshun
Ostara
Rainbow Serpent
Rhea
Yemaya

FIRE GODDESS
Brigid
Freya
Hestia
Pele

HEALER
Aine
Brigid
Cerridwen
Hathor
Hecate
Iris
Ix Chel
Rhiannon
Saraswati
Sekhmet
Tara

LOVE
Aine
Aphrodite
Branwen
Frigg
Hathor
Odudua
Oshun
Parvati
Selene
Xochiquetzal

MAGIC
Badb
Cerridwen
Hecate
Isis
The Morrigan
Nephthys
Oshun
Oya
Rhiannon
Selene

MARRIAGE
Frigg
Hera
Isis
Lakshmi
Mama Quilla
Parvati

MERCY/FORGIVENESS
Branwen
Kuan Yin
Rhiannon
Sita
Sophia
Tara

MOON GODDESS
Artemis
Chang'e
Ix Chel
Mama Quilla
Selene

PEACE/HARMONY
Hestia
Iris
Kuan Yin
Lakshmi
Ma'at
Odudua
Oshun
Parvati
Tara
White Buffalo Calf Woman

PROSPERITY
Anuket
Gaia
Lakshmi
Mami Wata
Odudua
Oshun
Wangmu Niangniang
White Buffalo Calf Woman

PROTECTION
Aditi
Aine
Bast
Durga
Hecate
Nephthys
Parvati
Shakti
Tara
Wangmu Niangniang

PURITY
Athena
Hestia
Kuan Yin
Saraswati
Tara

SEXUALITY
Aphrodite
Bast
Eos
Ishtar
Lilith
Xochiquetzal

SKY GODDESS
Eos
Iris
Nut
Odudua
Tefnut

SUN GODDESS
Amaterasu
Brigid
Eos
Sekhmet

TRUTH/JUSTICE
Ma'at
Nemesis
Oya
Sophia

WARRIOR GODDESS
Athena
Badb
Durga
Freya
Hera
Ishtar
Kali
Medb
The Morrigan
Nike
Sekhmet

WATER GODDESS
Anuket
Danu
Kuan Yin
Mami Wata
Oshun
Rainbow Serpent
Sedna
Tefnut
Tiamat
Yemaya

WISDOM
Athena
Ereshkigal
Freya
Hecate
Hestia
Lilith
Medb
Nephthys
Oshun
Saraswati
Sophia
Yemaya

IMAGE CREDITS

INDEX

ABOUT THE AUTHOR

Skye Alexander is the award-winning author of more than three dozen fiction and nonfiction books, including the popular Modern Witchcraft series. Her stories have been published in anthologies internationally, and her work has been translated into more than a dozen languages. She's also a feng shui practitioner, astrologer, artist, tarotist, and Reiki practitioner. The Discovery Channel featured her in the TV special *Secret Stonehenge* doing a ritual at Stonehenge. She divides her time between Texas and Massachusetts. Visit her at SkyeAlexander.com.